Travelling
To
Change Lives

PAUL BEAULIEU

Travelling
To
Change Lives

 Les Éditions
Mundo

Library and Archives Canada cataloguing in publication and Bibliothèque et Archives nationales du Québec

Beaulieu, Paul, 1950 December 30-

[Voyager pour changer des vies. English]

Travelling to change lives

Translation of : Voyager pour changer des vies.
Includes index.

ISBN 978-2-9814696-2

1. Beaulieu, Paul, 1950 December 30- - Travel. 2. Humanitarian assistance. 3. Voyages around the world. I. Title. II. Title : Voyager pour changer des vies. English.

HV544.5.B4213 2014 361.2'6092 C2014-942039-0

Translation:	Karen Hilchey
Revision and Proofreading:	James Ross
Computer graphics:	Hélène St-Cyr
Proofreading:	James Ross
Author's photographs:	Francis Vachon

Publishers:	Les éditions Mundo
	3223 Versant nord Blvd.
	Quebec City, (QC) G1X 3V5
	418 626-1308
Website:	www.editionsmundo.com
Copyright :	Paul Beaulieu
Legal deposit:	Bibliothèque et Archives nationales du Québec
	Archives Canada
ISBN:	Printed Version ISBN 978-2-9814696-2-5
	e-pub Version ISBN:978-2-9814696-3-2

Translated from the original French version: "Voyager pour changer des Vies", Editions Mundo September 2014

To my wife Aline for understanding my need
to travel.

To Rotary International who opened
the doors to the world.

**THE WORLD IS A BOOK,
AND THOSE WHO DO NOT TRAVEL
READ ONLY A SINGLE PAGE.**

(ST-AUGUSTINE)

INTRODUCTION

You like to travel? You have always wanted to see the world? Spending two weeks on the beach does not satisfy your need for discovery? There are numerous ways to travel and to come back home fulfilled, but nothing is more rewarding than to come back home with the feeling we were able to help the needy.

More and more people express the desire to go abroad one day to help the needy and to share their experience. People are retiring at a younger age and as life expectancy is longer all those years of retirement allow people to have many beautiful life projects.

There are also a whole bunch of young people who are looking for adventure and who want to change the world, while others want to pause in the middle of their career to catch their breath. Being a volunteer abroad is a good way to change your daily routine.

Such a project requires preparation. We need to know on which one to embark. Some could be surprised by their reactions the first time they find themselves in a difficult situation abroad. Rubbing shoulders with daily misery could very soon become unbearable. We must therefore learn in advance what to expect.

The lack of comfort can also play on your morale. In this type of trip, life conditions are not the same as they are at home and over the long haul that could prove to be difficult. Each day that goes by could increase the discomfort more than we could have imagined before leaving.

For those of us who have that sensitivity to international aid it is hard sometimes to find how we could be useful. We're not all doctors who can offer our help in disaster areas. We don't all have the capacity to leave for several months. So we have to find a way to use our talents. Personally, I found a way to get involved. I have developed an expertise in arranging financing for humanitarian projects, in monitoring and evaluating them for good stewardship.

I have realised my dream through Rotary International, an organisation made up of business people and professionals who want to be engaged in our society and who have the desire to change things. There are many organisations at the international level that offer the opportunity to get involved. It is therefore a question of finding the organisation that meets your needs and where you will be able to make use of your talents.

In this book, I relate some of the experiences I lived during these past fifteen years throughout my numerous trips to South America, Africa and Asian countries such as Mongolia and India. These stories are often moving, often funny, but mostly always instructive. Throughout these situations, you can imagine how you would have reacted.

These stories describe situations that I actually lived. If I had the chance, I would not hesitate for one moment to relive each of them again. Even if sometimes I was tired of those long trips, mostly done in difficult conditions, I was always eager to accept new missions. My suitcase was never far away and I always came back home with a head full of memories.

Talking about your trips in a book is not easy because the reader has not had the same experience and does not know the places or the people you visited. I hope you enjoy reading this book and, more importantly, if you ever feel like leaving, keep in mind that you can do it too. Meanwhile, I hope that reading this will allow you to travel in the comfort of your home.

1

THE BEGINNING OF A MAGNIFICENT ADVENTURE

One day, while traveling in Central America for several weeks in order to learn Spanish, my oldest son called home to give us some news. He recounted his journey and what he had seen and, above all, he described to us the poverty which had unsettled him. All of a sudden, he said to me: "You know Papa, the Third World is not here. It is our home, because more than two-thirds of the population of the world live in poverty." This sentence struck me. My son had just realised how fortunate he was to live in a rich country like Canada. This was his first trip abroad, thus his first real contact with the poverty of the countries in Central America. Up until then, he had lived in a peaceful haven where he enjoyed what most of us would consider being the good life. As a parent, I suddenly realised that my son had become an adult who had discovered the world beyond his own fortunate circumstances. In a few words, he had described the reality of the world in which we were living.

Several people have had the opportunity to travel to the most beautiful places on earth. Very often, they get off the plane in a hurry and rush into an air-conditioned bus, which brings them to a holiday resort. There, they enjoy beautiful beaches without having to leave their hotel grounds, so they remain largely unaware of all that is happening around them. As one of my good friends used to say: "They travel, but they don't land anywhere!"

As for me, I have decided that once I land somewhere, I will go and explore.

I have to mention that at a very young age I became aware of the suffering in impoverished countries. A missionary uncle at the White Fathers in Africa gave me an account of what was happening there. At school, the nuns spoke to us about their missions abroad, but like most others, I was content to watch the various occurrences of famine presented to us on television. We have all heard about the famine in China in the late fifties and the famine in Biafra in the late sixties, which had horrified the whole world, because for the first time, we were able to witness the suffering from the comfort of our living room. Afterwards, there was Sahel, Somalia, Sudan and still today Niger and Darfur. Not to mention the suffering in the countries of sub-Sahel where famine is endemic.

Despite knowing all that was happening in the world, I would certainly never have done more than what I had already been doing up until then, if it had not been for my involvement in Rotary International. Rotary is a service club with a considerable amount of commitment in the world. Through its foundation, Rotary International conducts annual humanitarian projects of all kinds in which it invests several hundreds of millions of dollars. Moreover, Rotary is engaged in the campaign to eradicate poliomyelitis, in which it has invested to date more than one billion American dollars.

Thanks to Rotary, doors to the world were opening for me. After having become a member of the Quebec–Charlesbourg Rotary Club in 1993, I started to progress in the organisation. The more I discovered all that Rotary was doing, the more I was convinced that I could do the same, albeit in a small a way, in light of all that society had given me. After having been president of my club, I subsequently engaged myself at the district level (District 7790) where I became governor in 2002. This district regrouped fifty-six clubs in Eastern Quebec and the central part of the State of Maine.

Each year in our district we are used to realising an international project. The first project in which I was involved was in 1999 – 2000 with governor Beryl "Buffy" Sutherland. She had decided to help some families in Brazil, who were living in the dumps, having only cardboard boxes and metal sheets, which they managed to find to shelter themselves. Buffy, of whom I had become the right-hand man, had asked me to help her introduce a low-cost shelter construction project to members of all the clubs in our District. Originally, her plan was to build twenty-five such houses. During a discussion with her, I convinced her to present the project in such a way that each club would finance one house. Initially, the cost of one house had been evaluated at US $2,000. Each club would then be able to subsidize one house by donating $2,000 to the project. In this way, we would be able to consider building at least fifty houses instead of the twenty-five, which Buffy had foreseen at the beginning.

The project was presented during a training session for future club presidents. As soon as Buffy's presentation was finished, I made a speech thanking the governor and I took the opportunity to invite the clubs to subscribe to this exceptional project. It did not take long to receive a response. Very soon, one club president stood up and announced that he would get personally involved on behalf of his club and donate $2,000. Another one followed suit and then again another... Monetary contributions in the amount of $1,000, $2,000, and even one of $5,000 were made right on the spot. A considerable number of other clubs declared that they would keep us informed about the amount of their monetary contribution as soon as they discussed it with their board of directors. At the end of the meeting, we had already consolidated an amount of $37,000. Governor Buffy was simply ecstatic. By adding the subsidies which we were able to collect from the Rotary Foundation of Rotary International, we realised that it would be possible to construct at least seventy-five houses for these homeless families in Brazil. With an average of four people per family, this represented over three hundred people for whom we would be able to provide accommodations!

It is then that I became aware of the power resulting from the participation of many people, and I realised that with the help of the Rotary Foundation, we were capable of accomplishing gigantic projects. Remarkably, working together we were able to shelter a family for half the price of a garden shed! Several members of our clubs also realised that for a sum as modest as $2,000, it was possible to provide a family with a roof over their head. In the end, we succeeded in building a total of one hundred and thirty-seven houses! For me, this was for me the beginning of a magnificent adventure and since then, I have been involved in all kinds of projects. For our Rotary district, this was the beginning of many years of involvement in international sponsorship projects and this involvement still continues.

The following year, Governor Jean-Hugues Laflamme presented a proposal to help an orphanage in Bacău, Romania. The country had just lived through the Ceausescu regime and a number of State orphanages were abandoned with no resources. The plan consisted of endowing an orphanage, which was run by the nuns, with a trade school and farming equipment, so that by educating the young orphans in agriculture, they could become self-sufficient in feeding themselves. The project also consisted of installing a library and a computer room. To introduce the proposal to the club presidents, we used the same approach as the previous year and, again, they demonstrated a strong enthusiasm by immediately subscribing. Including the funds donated by the Foundation of Rotary International, we were able to achieve everything for around US$117,000. The Casa of Copii then became one of the best equipped orphanages in Romania.

These repeated successes were proof that we were able to carry out important projects with the help of our clubs and the Rotary Foundation. As it was now my turn to be chosen to be the governor of our Rotary district, it was up to me to search for a project in which we could get involved. After the successes of the past two years, I wanted to achieve something which would once again, thanks to our action, make a difference to a significant number of people.

I was busy preparing my mandate for the year as District Governor, when one day I learned that one of my club members, a professor by trade, was preparing for a month-long trip to Peru with a group of students. I knew that he was in contact with the members of a Rotary Club in Arequipa in the southern part of that country, so I asked him to get information from the Rotarians in this club with regard to a potential project that we could carry out together. I indicated to him a certain number of parameters which appeared important to me: the idea had to come from the local population, the project would be expected to have a long-term impact on the population and would fall within a budget of US$125,000.

A month later, the day after he returned, Jean-Pierre called me to tell me that he had something to show me. I could sense his enthusiasm at the other end of the line. We made an appointment to meet for breakfast the next day. This would be the beginning of a tremendous adventure for me!

2

PERU

My First Project

In mid-December 2001, Jean-Pierre and I flew to Arequipa, Peru, in order to investigate the feasibility of the project he had presented to me in August upon returning from his journey. This was an extensive project; it was therefore important for us to go on-site in order to have a better idea and to meet our future partners. The proposal consisted of creating an agricultural institute in the southern part of the country. The idea had originated from Melva Pinto, a member of the Arequipa Club and a native of the Pacific Coast, an isolated region, which was a two-hour drive from the big city. It was impossible for the children of poverty-stricken families in this region to pursue their studies because to do so would require them to live in Arequipa, which was well beyond their means.

This was my first journey to South America and to a developing country. I had taken some Spanish courses a few years earlier, but the company of Jean-Pierre reassured me: he was fluent in Spanish. On the airplane, a song kept running through my mind: *Bésame, Bésame mucho…* I asked Jean-Pierre what the lyrics meant. He burst into laughter and translated them for me: "Kiss me, kiss me hard". He would not stop bringing up this joke throughout the journey… I can assure you that by that time I had come to know the lyrics of this song by heart, and likewise their meaning!

Around 11 pm, after travelling for more than ten hours, we landed in Lima where we would be staying overnight. For me, this was culture shock. Upon leaving the customs and immigration area, we were literally gobbled up by a human tide, which had been waiting for the travellers. In the overheated terminal building, two to three thousand people were waiting for passengers coming from the United States on three airplanes arriving at nearly the same time. Struggling to drag my suitcase behind me, I followed Jean-Pierre as best I could as he disappeared into the dense crowd. The throng of people parted a little to let him pass and then formed again right behind him. I elbowed my way through the crowd and finally arrived outside where a bunch of taxi drivers closed in around us. I finally caught up with Jean-Pierre who was already negotiating the price of the ride to Miraflores where we would be spending the night.

In Lima, there are no hotels near the airport. We had to go to this affluent suburb of the capital where hotels and buildings overlooking the Pacific were concentrated. After a thirty-minute ride, we arrived at our hotel. We left our luggage in the room, and even though it was almost midnight, we were starved so we decided to go out and grab a bite before going to bed. As people in southern countries traditionally eat late, we were certain that we would be able to find some restaurants that would be still open. How pleasant it was to be able to stroll along the streets at this hour without our boots and heavy coats! In the park, there stood an enormous Christmas tree decorated with gifts. This reminded us that we were only a few days from Christmas.

The next day, we took a plane to Arequipa, our final destination. There, we were greeted by a group of local Rotary Club members who invited to breakfast at one of the posh restaurants in the city. We ate in a grandiose courtyard where flowers abounded. An orchestra played music from the Andes. The atmosphere was very pleasant. My limited Spanish prevented me from understanding all that was happening, but Jean-Pierre helped me with the translation.

Jean-Pierre would be staying with one of his friends, Melvin. The club president Edmee and her husband Pepe were absolutely determined to have me stay at their place, which meant that I would have to live without my companion who had been my interpreter until then. I kept my dictionary close at hand, which then became "my new best friend". Upon arrival at their place, they offered me to sleep in their young son's room. I undid my luggage and got into the bed which fitted tightly next to the window. I would have to get used to my new accommodations. In the bathroom, a trickle of water was all that was available from the shower tap. No hot water, so I had to content myself with a minute stream of cool water. I would have to get used to living with this shortage, but tired as I was from the long hours of travel, the moment I lay down I forgot all about it and I fell asleep almost immediately.

A Project to Accomplish

The next day, Mauricio, a member of the Club, came to pick us up. He spoke a little French which he had learned while he was a student in Paris. He supervised a medical centre, which he had helped to establish in one of the destitute neighbourhoods of the city. He was very proud to have us visit his centre, although it was not yet completely ready. He explained to us in great detail how each single pill was closely monitored. All the medication received by the clinic and given to the patients was recorded. All these procedures were performed manually. Other than the clinic where physicians from town took turns to come work several hours a week, the centre included a lounge and a mutual aid area for the families. Upstairs, a space had been reserved to install a kitchen where women would be taught how to prepare healthy and more affordable meals. Another room had also been reserved to provide meals for the children. Unfortunately, there was not enough money to purchase the necessary kitchen equipment. For the moment, this proposed community kitchen project was only a big empty room with a cement floor and walls made of concrete blocks. We found ourselves in the middle of an unfinished construction site. I asked Mauricio how much they would need to finish his project. He explained that with $2,000, he would be able to purchase the kitchen equipment, as well as the chairs and the tables needed to feed the children. Only two thousand dollars! This amount seemed ridiculously small, given all the benefits given the fact that it would enable the children to satisfy their appetite at lunchtime.

I realised that this amount, which seemed relatively modest to us, was considered to be almost astronomical in this country. Without making any promises to Mauricio, I decided that I would look for the money needed to help him finish his project. After all, it should be fairly easy to raise two thousand dollars in our country.

Upon my return, I approached my colleagues and my friends to raise the funds. I suggested to them an amount of $100 for what had become "my" project! I soon realised that it was not that easy to raise money for a project abroad. First of all, Peru was a country about which little was known in Canada. Secondly, people responded to me with the stock phrase "In our country, we also have poverty". Excellent reason to avoid contributing! Others, however, donated with a smile, knowing that this donation would go directly to those in need. An anonymous person even donated $500 with the simple intention to help. I did not know who he was, nor did he know who I was, but he had generously donated after learning from us that the money would be remitted entirely to the centre.

During this quest for money, I had had some beautiful surprises such as this anonymous donor, but also some disappointments. The biggest disappointment came from a colleague to whom I had described what I had witnessed. This man, who earned a salary way above that of a prime minister, told me initially that he only donated to The United Way. Afterwards, he came up with all sorts of excuses to avoid donating anything in the end.

This anecdote allowed me to soon realise that we were living in a world where priorities do not always take into consideration the needs of people living in less privileged countries. We spend an enormous amount of money on entertainment, while elsewhere others often do not have any food to eat. I understand that we are not obliged to offer our help. I also understand that we do not have to deprive ourselves in order to help the very poor, but the lack of compassion of some saddened me. Nevertheless, the thought of this man, who had donated $500 without any hesitation, comforted me. Three months after my return, the two thousand dollars had been raised and the money had been sent to Peru enabling Mauricio to complete his mission.

After having visited the centre with Mauricio, we caught up with the others for a visit to the city of Arequipa, also known as the White City. I slowly got accustomed to their rhythm of life. My eyes were wide open. At the Plaza de Armas, I noticed the damage done to the cathedral by two big earthquakes occurring in the summer of 2001. One of the two prominent bell towers had crashed to the ground. Fortunately, the rest of the city seemed not to have suffered excessively. The day passed by swiftly and we planned to leave very early the next morning for the region of Mollendo on the Pacific Coast, where the project was to be implemented.

The next day, I got up at 6 am, because we had to catch a bus for Mollendo at 7 am. After a quick breakfast, we jumped into a taxi. In Arequipa, catching a taxi did not require much of an effort. That morning, while waiting for Edmee, the sheer number of little yellow taxis passing by the house amused me. I estimated an average of eleven taxis per minute. All we had to do was get closer to the street and immediately a taxi would stop. Upon arrival at the station, we rejoined the group. Apart from Edmee and me, there was Melvin, her daughter, Melva, and Jean-Pierre who got up late and had forgotten to put on his glasses! Melvin's daughter jumped into a taxi and went back for them. She returned as we were about to get on the bus.

The bus was already full. I took a seat. Surprisingly, the bench was broken and apparently, I would have to suffer the whole journey without being able to rest on the back of the seat as it was loose. But I could live with that. When Edmee saw how uncomfortably I was seated, she insisted on changing seats with me. She explained to me that, being a lot smaller than me, she would be able to cope better with the situation. Seated on my new bench, I tried to look through the window, but the glass was so dirty that it was difficult to see anything. As the sun was already high in the sky, people drew the curtains to prevent the sun from overheating the bus, which was not air-conditioned. This made it difficult to see the landscape which seemed very desert-like, yet very beautiful. After a two-hour ride, we finally arrived at Mollendo next to the Pacific.

As soon as we arrived in the little town, we headed for downtown in order to meet the sub-prefect of the region who was appointed by the Government of Lima to manage an administrative region. He welcomed us warmly and gave us permission to visit the buildings that my friends were longing to see and which could potentially be used to house the Agricultural Institute. The sub-prefect expressed to us his strong belief in education as it was necessary for local development and he assured us of his utmost support.

For him, establishing a school dedicated to agriculture was needed to benefit the region. Our meeting would be the first and last time we would see him. A few months after our visit, he was dismissed from his office. The Peruvian Government had decided to elect a president in each region in order to decentralize the power of the State.

A School Full of Danger

Before leaving Mollendo for the region farther south, where we were considering implementing our project, I was invited to visit a school for handicapped children, the only one of its kind in the whole region, I was told. It did not take me long to understand that they would ask me for money in order to help this school.

After being greeted by the principal upon arrival, the children were asked to line up in the playground. The teachers made them sing in our honour and then they showed me around the school. The classrooms were small and minimally equipped. In a hidden part of the playground, I caught a glimpse of a space open to the sky, wedged between the main building and the fence: the kitchen! The food was stored on shelves and there was a small double-burner gas stove on the floor. A big bowl of rice was sitting directly on the beaten earth floor... Everything was in the open air; thus the place was vulnerable to the invasion of flies. Even though local living conditions were not comparable to ours, I think that there is nevertheless a limit.

There were many more surprises in store for me. In another room, which I was told served as a physiotherapy room, there was a woman who was busy helping a child of four or five years stretch his legs. The child was lying down on a wooden table with no mattress. I did not see any physiotherapy device. Having already visited this type of centre, I knew that specialized devices are normally used to optimize treatments. I knew nothing about physiotherapy, but I found this treatment room to be in a state of extreme destitution.

In another corner of the playground, I was able to notice some swings whose metal frames were secured in cement blocks.

The problem was that the cement bases presented some thirty centimetres of rough surface, making the children very vulnerable to being injured. In our country, such a situation would be totally unacceptable. I concluded my visit by telling myself that this centre for handicapped children needed a little help... This was my second visit to a centre for children in two days and once again I felt challenged.

Once more, I made the commitment that upon returning to my country, I would do something to improve this school. As this required more money than what was needed for the kitchen in the community centre, it would be necessary for one or more clubs to be willing to fund this project. Five years later, in 2006, the Quebec Club and its partners, the Nanterre Club in France and the Bologna Club in Italy, accepted to fund this project with donations amounting to $15,000. By taking into account the formalities and the implementation time, it was expected that by June 2008, everything would be completed. For me, it would be very satisfying to provide these young handicapped children with a specialized learning environment that was also secure and pleasant. It took six and a half years to complete the project, but the important thing was that the project had finally been accomplished.

I returned in July 2008 to oversee the work which had been done. The kitchen finally resembled a proper one, the swings were safe, the playground had been refurbished, but above all, the rooms now contained some brand new rehabilitation equipment as well as some colourful toys to assist the physical development of these children. Needless to say, the principal of the school, the one who had greeted us six years ago, welcomed me with a big smile. I was privileged to be embraced by all the teachers and the children who offered me their songs as a heartfelt gesture of gratitude.

Protocol, Protocol!

It was time to leave the centre for handicapped children in Mollendo for the coastal villages. In the village of *La Curba*, we were brought to visit a government-owned building, situated at the centre of the small village. From there, we went to meet the mayor who welcomed us into the Great Hall of his City Council. I was amazed by the prevailing formalities. After having discussed how the Institute would be managed and, more importantly, its location, we committed ourselves by signing a "*convenio*", a memorandum of understanding between the Yanuhara-Arequipa Rotary Club and the municipality of La Curba. After having formalized everything on paper, I was presented a plaque thanking me on behalf of the municipality for my support and nominating me as "Distinguished Honorary Citizen". I was not too sure how to react. After all, I had not done anything yet and the project was far from being completed. Nevertheless, I accepted the plaque, which now hangs on the wall in my home office.

The three-storey building proposed to us was used as a warehouse. The place was dirty and there was dust everywhere. The backyard was cluttered with debris of all sorts. How could one seriously imagine turning this building into a school? As for my hosts, they seemed thrilled to have found such a place. It would take a lot of work to transform it into an acceptable building, but the Rotarians were ready to do anything in order to see the birth of this Agricultural Institute. They looked at this building in a different way. The comfort of our North American schools was inconceivable to them. But, since they would be the ones with the heaviest task in the project, I did not discourage them despite my skepticism.

Our next stop was in another village where we gave out clothes prepared by the group of Rotarians from the Yanuhara-Arequipa Club. In addition to the clothes, we also distributed a chocolate-flavoured soya drink to the children. While the mothers were choosing the clothes, the children headed off for the chocolate drink. The orderly manner of the children surprised me: they waited quietly for their turn. I must mention that they were impressed by our presence, as we were strangers to them, and they looked at us with eyes wide open. For them, it was a festive day! Very soon, the boxes were empty.

After that meeting, we headed straight to the neighbouring municipality of *La Meja,* where they were eager to show us a field where the future students would conduct their experiments. We stopped in front of the town hall. On seeing us arrive, a fanfare of musicians started playing music. The Mayor was there to greet us and together we proceeded, in a parade and to the sound of the fanfare, toward his office on the second floor. The fanfare followed us everywhere. A cameraman from a local television channel walked backwards in front of us filming the event. I felt like a politician in front of a pack of journalists. However, I had not yet done anything to deserve such a treatment and so many honours. Then it dawned on me that it was not Paul Beaulieu who was being greeted in this manner, but the governor of a Rotary district who had the authority and the financial means to help bring to this little municipality the Agricultural Institute so desperately needed in the region.

We ended up discussing the project in the Mayor's office. After five minutes, he invited us to follow him to the field that his municipality would like to propose to us. As soon as we started walking, the orchestra resumed playing music. Outside, other municipal officials were waiting for us. We hurried into the Mayor's car whereas another group stood up at the back of a small red pickup truck. In this group, I met a young man from Cap-Rouge, near Quebec City, who was staying in the region as part of a student exchange program. He was happy to be able to meet someone from his country. He accompanied us throughout the day.

We visited the field. I knew absolutely nothing about it then, but they seemed to be saying to us that it was fertile. I had to make a leap of faith. After all, they were the ones to benefit from this field, so they had probably made a good choice. The discussions lasted for many minutes under the blazing sun. We talked about what we could do with the old building still standing on the land. It was agreed that once renovated, it would make a good shed for the tools. When we got back to the car, I was covered with dust, my shoes were not black anymore but grey and I was very sweaty, not being used to this heat.

Afterwards, we headed toward another field. Passing in front of city hall, our procession stopped for a few moments to allow the Mayor to get a document. As soon as they caught sight of us, the musicians, who had been sitting quietly in the shade, grabbed their instruments and began playing. Unfortunately for them, we left before they could even finish their first piece! We visited another field, but this time things went faster. Everyone was hungry and we ended up in the only restaurant in the village for my first meal in the Peruvian countryside. The walls of the restaurant were made of bamboo strips through which the dust from passing cars seeped in. At least, we were in the shade. They strongly recommended the fish. My companion Jean-Pierre opted for a meat dish, a local speciality. He was used to this food, as he visited Peru once or twice a year. My fish, which had been cooked on a grill "a la plancha", was absolutely delicious. As we were on the shore of the ocean, there was daily supply of fresh fish.

After the meal, we were informed that we must return to *La Curba* in order to meet the Mayor again, because they had discovered an error in the *convenio*. As he was not able to receive us straight away, we stopped at the beach for a little rest. Our young Canadian student seized the opportunity to jump in the ocean. Although the water was not very warm, it was warmer than the Atlantic and our young Quebecker was proud to show the Peruvians that a Canadian was able to swim in cold water! They invited me to do the same, but I declined. We had just witnessed a beautiful demonstration and I did not want to overshadow this brave young man.

After having redone the *convenio*, we still had a few moments before taking the bus back to Arequipa. The Mayor invited us to the local event of the week: a cockfight. I was not really interested in attending, but curiosity got the better of me. We were driven to a building which was located a short distance from the village. Inside, at least two hundred people were seated around a sort of arena. They brought in the cocks which were blindfolded. Some razor-sharp blades were attached to their feet. Seeing this, it was easy for me to imagine what would happen next! This kind of event is not for the fainted-hearted. As the cockfighting began, there was a lot of blood. The scene was simply horrifying. Thankfully, it was time to leave and someone came to take us away from there. I was glad to leave this crowd that screamed with excitement each time it saw some blood.

We Travelled First-Class!

We took the bus back to Arequipa. There were some seats available. Many farmers only purchased standing places to save a bit of money. Jean-Pierre and I seated ourselves in the middle of the bus. In the aisle next to us stood a mother and her little daughter, who was around five years old. At first, I did not understand why they remained standing. I thought that they did not have a long way to go and that they would be getting off soon in one of these little villages that I was able to catch a glimpse of earlier along the way. When we left Mollendo, it was getting dark. The bus was crowded and the aisle was full. It was nearly 9 pm. As the time passed, the little girl showed increasing signs of fatigue. I felt uncomfortable to see this mother and her child standing and almost losing their balance at each curve the bus took. Jean-Pierre explained to me that they would probably make the whole journey like this, standing in the aisle, having paid for the less expensive places. The little girl could hardly keep her eyes open. They were constantly shoved by other people bigger than them, who were also swaying from side to side with each jolt of the ride.

Jean-Pierre attempted to approach the little girl. At first, she hardly responded to him, but as she was very tired, she finally accepted to sit on my companion's knees. Soon afterwards, she fell asleep and only reopened her eyes once they reached their destination, two hours later. The mother picked up her child and, after thanking Jean-Pierre timidly, she disappeared in the crowd of travellers. For me, this was another culture shock to see first-hand the difference between the rich and the poor. For the first time, I felt very rich compared to those around me and the privileges of being rich put me ill at ease. I was embarrassed to be in such comfort while all these poor people had to endure this difficult situation, which I had a hard time to accept. This would not be the last time I had such a feeling during my travels. The next day, I would have to go through an even more difficult experience, which would challenge my values with respect to poverty.

A Hospital, No Equipment!

To carry out the Agricultural Institute project, members of the Rotary Club had contacted the Universidad Nacional San Augustin (UNSA). We met the rector to inform him about the efforts we had made the previous day and to establish an agreement between them and the Arequipa Rotary Club. We were received in a ceremonial conference room. At the centre of the room was a huge wooden table. Along the walls, there were about forty chairs with high backs carved in wood. The room was sumptuous. I was spellbound by the richness and the beauty of this room. A group of journalists was already there to attend the press conference given by Dr. Cornejo, the rector of the University who was to announce the Agricultural Institute project.

The director of public relations at the University, a rather tall man, compared to the Peruvians who are generally quite short, read aloud in a booming voice the long *convenio* prepared by the University to officialise our collaboration. Undoubtedly, here, nothing is done without a *convenio*. This made me uncomfortable, as we were far from having a well-crafted project. The buildings we had seen the previous day were in poor condition and there were still some details to be worked out. Furthermore, at this stage, I did not feel I had the authority to sign the agreements on behalf of my Rotary district.

As soon as the solemn reading of the three-to-four-page *convenio* was finished, I was invited along with the Yahuara-Arequipa Club President, Edmee Romero Barientes, to join the rector seated at a huge table facing the conference table. This was the moment to sign the famous document. As soon as we were seated, the director of public relations, who had just finished reading the document, presented to Edmee and me a copy which we were to sign and then initial each page. As soon as we started signing, the photographers triggered their devices and started clicking their cameras. Afterwards, the rector delivered a press conference to explain the project in greater detail. They tried to interview me, but my very limited Spanish put an end almost immediately to their questions. Jean-Pierre responded on my behalf.

We were then invited to the rector's office for a private discussion. From what I understood later, this was considered to be a great honour in Peru. There was a row of armchairs facing the rector's massive desk. They had me seated in one of these armchairs alongside Jean-Pierre and Edmee. The two or three others who were accompanying us as well as the rector's assistants, around ten of them, were standing behind us. They brought us some soft drinks while we were waiting for the rector to finish his interviews. When he arrived, he sat behind the desk and began with the least formal part of the meeting. He talked to us about how he had come to appreciate Canada because of a colloquium he had attended and he expressed his gratitude to us for the project we wanted to achieve. He described the university projects to us with an emphasis on the university hospital whose construction had already been undertaken a few years ago. As the University was not wealthy, the construction progressed at the pace of incoming funds. The rector foresaw that the construction would be completed the following year. Then, what remained to be done would be to equip and to furnish the hospital.

Jean-Pierre then mentioned to him an organisation in Quebec, Collaboration Santé Internationale, which collects used material from hospitals in Quebec, restores them to good condition and dispatches them to developing countries. Each week, this organisation ships at least one forty-foot container abroad. The rector was interested in this offer and decided to organise for us a private visit to the hospital under construction. We arranged to meet the next morning at 10 am. The University would provide a bus to take us to the building site, in a suburb far from downtown.

There, we discovered a modern hospital in its original architecture. The building was situated at the centre of a huge tract of land, which would be turfed and would, as such, become the only greenish isle in this poor area. We began our visit, accompanied by the rector of the Faculty of Medicine. The hospital was a big, two-storey cement building in the shape of a star. The nurses' stations were located at the centre, thus reducing the travel distance for the medical staff. The project was impressive, but unfortunately, they were not able to give us a likely inauguration date, as they did not have enough funds to finish it.

In the summer of 2002, a delegation from the University came to Quebec City so they could verify the material which Collaboration Santé Internationale was able to put at their disposal. For two days, they would go back and forth to the warehouses in order to choose the needed equipment. A few weeks later, a container would be dispatched, filled with hospital beds, bedroom furniture and an array of medical devices, ranging from a baby incubator to sterilizing devices as well as the necessary material to equip a dentist's office.

That same day, on the way back from visiting the hospital, I would live through an experience, which would change forever the way I perceive the world. The Rotary Club members who were accompanying us showed the bus driver an address and asked him to stop there for a couple of minutes, the time needed for a short visit to someone whom the Club had been helping for several months. They wanted to show me one of their involvements in their community.

Real Misery ...

A few months ago, a woman had been assaulted by some thieves on a street in Arequipa. After beating her, they abandoned her on the street. This mother of two had to be hospitalized for several weeks. Her story was published in the newspapers and the Yanuhara Rotary Club decided to help this woman.

The bus entered a street lined with rows of cement walls, hiding the courtyard of the houses and projecting a sense of melancholy and monotonousness. After arriving at destination, the Rotarians got off the bus and asked me to follow them. We entered the courtyard of the house. In reality, the courtyard was only a space surrounded by walls made of grey cement blocks over which were some fragments of glass, offering a modest protection against possible intruders. Edmee headed directly toward the house, knocked at the door and entered without waiting for an answer. Everyone followed her, and so did I. The house consisted of a single room. A woman was seated in a wheelchair at the far end of the room. The President engaged her in conversation. My limited Spanish prevented me from understanding what they were saying to each other. The woman spoke between sobs when the President tried to encourage her.

Meanwhile, I surveyed the one and only room of this house. A simple bed was set up along a wall with two smaller beds along the opposite wall, apparently for the children. At one end of the room was a shelf with some clothes. Next to it, another little shelf was used as a bookshelf for a few books. There were no toys, no other furniture except for a little round stove against the wall facing me. Together with a few pots near the stove, they formed the kitchen corner. I saw nothing which indicated to me that there was running water or a bathroom. Only one window opened to the internal courtyard, but there again we could only see cement walls. What a sad world!

They explained to me that this woman, without any resources, had become depressed because of her assault. This I could understand because, being confined in her wheelchair, her entire world seemed to be this sombre room and this dismal courtyard. Edmee did all she could to encourage her, but her efforts seemed to be in vain. In front of so much destitution, a sudden feeling of uselessness arose within me. What could I do to help her? I had some money in my pocket… If I gave her $100, she would be able to improve her living conditions, but would she feel insulted by my offer? Would this be a wise solution?

I tried to mull it over, but I did not manage to convince myself to take the money out of my pocket. I slid my hand into the pocket, twiddled with the notes, but something held me back. This was not a question of money, far from it. I felt so rich compared to her. No, I feared that I would come across as some wealthy visitor who was showing off his riches by throwing a few dollars at this woman. I hesitated and held back. I felt more and more utterly useless and helpless in front of the situation. For the first time, I was facing tangible poverty and I searched deeply within myself as to what was the best thing to do. Finally, the group left the house and we returned to the bus.

I was overwhelmed. When we were back on the road, I continued to question myself. How would I have been able to help this woman and her two children? Had I done well? I couldn't shake the doubt. The Rotary Club was coming to her assistance and this comforted me. It was not the first time I witnessed misery, but this was the first time I felt so devastated. Perhaps, the reason was that for once, I was truly concerned about it. Was it because this time, I would have been able to respond directly to help this person? I did not know and I still have not found a satisfactory answer. Of course, I had found some answers, but were they the right ones?

I came to the conclusion that, for me, the best course of action was to continue with others in our joint efforts to build projects for the benefit of those in need. By combining our efforts, we could transform the lives of several hundred, indeed several thousands of people. I have been a Rotary Club member for over a decade, but I had been transformed into a true Rotarian in this woman's house.

This visit remained engraved in my memory. I would never forget that moment when I realised how fortunate I was in life and how some people were in dire need of help. Of course, I knew all this before, but there, I felt it in the depths of my being. I would never be the same again and I would no longer view life in the same light. Unknowingly, this lady had transformed my life far more than what I would have been able to do for her by giving her a small amount of money. Although years have passed, I can still clearly visualize her seated in her wheelchair in the middle of her small house, grey and gloomy, and each time this image encourages me to keep doing what I am doing.

The next day was our departure day. We had to take a plane back to Lima and return home. The day began with breakfast at President Edmee's house. For the occasion of this last morning, they cooked me a special meal: a rice dish with fish. The smell of fish coming from the kitchen blew me away. I was served my dish and I admit that, at the time, I wondered how I would be able to eat fish so early in the morning. In order to please my hosts, I had a taste of it and once the shock passed, the rice turned out to be absolutely delicious. When in Rome, do as the Romans do, as the saying goes! I just lived a beautiful and concrete example of this saying. I would relive this experience the following year during a trip to Ecuador.

After a visit to the market to buy some souvenirs to bring back home, we went downtown for the club meeting. An exception had been made to reschedule the weekly meeting to noon on this day in order that both of us, Jean-Pierre and I, would be able to meet all the members. More than thirty people attended the meeting. During the formal section of the meal, in order to thank me for being so enthusiastic in supporting their Agricultural Institute project and to encourage me to continue to support them by subsidizing the project through our Rotary district, they took the opportunity to honour me. They asked me to come to the front next to the President who was already on the stage.

From the very end of the room, I saw two little girls of four or five years moving towards me, dressed in long white dresses with a golden halo over their head and some little wings in the back. They were little angels. They moved toward me, carrying a frame assigning me as the Angel of the Yanuhara-Arequipa Rotary Club. I was very touched to have been given so many honours. My eyes watered. I felt that it would not be possible for me to disappoint these people who placed so much hope in me.

The President Gets Involved Personally

When I returned to Peru just over two years later, things had changed. The original project had evolved and so had the political framework. The Peruvian Government had decided to replace the regional sub-prefect by some regional presidents duly elected by the local population. The new president of the province of Arequipa, Daniel Vera Ballon, was an energetic man who put his heart into the economic development of his province. He believed in the importance of education and the idea of establishing a higher-level Agricultural Institute fascinated him to the point where he committed himself to pay for the construction of the school and to allocate the land for free. This good fortune of having President Daniel Vera Ballon involved in the Institute project was due to the fact that his secretary, who was also the sister of former Club President Edmee Romero, had made him aware of it.

To celebrate my return, the Yanuhara-Arequipa Rotary Club members organised a ground-breaking ceremony with President Vera Ballon. Around ten people from Quebec accompanied me, one of which was Jean-Pierre who had served as my guide during my first trip. We took the opportunity to visit the marvellous Inca site of Machu Picchu before arriving Arequipa. During my trips, I had had the opportunity to visit a number of places, each as beautiful as the next, but none had impressed me as much as Machu Picchu. The site itself is absolutely grandiose and is a must for anyone visiting Peru. All the group members have a lasting memory of this visit. How could we forget such a unique site where an advanced civilization had dwelled? Without their obvious knowledge of astronomy, the Incas would not have been able to construct such a city.

The day following our arrival at Arequipa, our entire group left very early in the morning along with our Rotarian friends to visit the little village of Cocachacra, where the Institute would eventually be built. On the bus, the two groups took turns to sing songs from their respective countries. The journey was delightful and it spawned a beautiful comradeship amongst us. Upon arrival at our destination, a formal lunch had been organised with the President of the province and the mayors of surrounding municipalities.

During this formal lunch, my spouse Aline was seated beside me opposite some mayors of the region. Amongst themselves, they were commenting in Spanish on her beautiful blue eyes, convinced that she would not understand them. Imagine their surprise when an Arequipa Club member who was accompanying us came to say a few words in Spanish to her and she responded in the same language! This just goes to show that you must always be cautious when making comments. As it seemed that the Institute project was very likely to carry on, following my first trip, Aline and I enrolled in Spanish courses, which allowed us, from that moment onward, to understand what was happening around us.

After lunch, our entire delegation went to the site where the future school would be erected. Political signs announced the passage of the President who, at that time, was blessed with very strong support from the local population. An improvised platform was set up on a small hill and, after the official speeches of the Mayor and the President, it was my turn to make a speech as a representative of Rotary International. I addressed the crowd with my uncertain Spanish. On the bus which had brought us to the Valley of Tambo, my Peruvian friends had helped me prepare my speech. I imagine that my pronunciation was acceptable since people applauded at the right moments!

In Peru, to officialise the beginning of work, a bottle of sparkling wine was suspended from a tripod, which I had the honour of breaking with a hammer. Not wanting to fail, I struck the bottle quite firmly and succeeded in splashing everyone, even the parish priest who was standing too close for that matter! Afterward, President Vera Ballon and I mixed a symbolic spadesful of cement on the foundations of the future Institute.

Since Peruvians are very formal, we then had to go to the village school for another ceremony with the Notables in front of the population of the region. Here again, speeches were made and this time I had to improvise in Spanish, not having been warned in advance that I would have to make a speech. My accent must have been terrible, because it was not until the very end that people applauded politely. But no matter, my goal was not to become a politician, but to achieve a project which was very dear to me.

The President took the opportunity to invite everyone in our group that same evening to Arequipa for the opening ceremony of a church which had to be restored after having suffered severe damage during the earthquakes of 2001. As he had been the one to approve the implementation of the Institute and authorize the construction of some new buildings, we could hardly refuse. We knew that we were going to be politically instrumental to him in this event, but we did not have much choice, so we promised to attend.

After the President had left, our group boarded a bus to bring us back to Arequipa. Before leaving, several people who attended the ceremony insisted on shaking our hand to thank us for having contributed to the implementation of what would be the only Institute of Superior Education in their region. This meant that their children would not have to go to Arequipa. Like most people in the region, who barely managed to survive on agriculture, very few of them could afford to send their children to be educated outside the region.

As I had guessed, President Vera Ballon made use of our presence to boost his popularity that evening. When we arrived at the church, a large crowd had already gathered. Curious onlookers were quickly shoved aside in order to make room for us. Even the parish priest would see himself pushed back a few rows. When it was his turn, the President was warmly applauded and a crowd of admirers followed him to the place of honour. Once installed, he looked around to make sure that we were there. He greeted me before getting on the platform located right beside the church.

In his speech, the President took the opportunity to highlight the credits of his administration, which was responsible for the renovation of the church damaged by the earthquakes. He also took the opportunity to explain our presence by mentioning the Agricultural Institute project as a joint achievement with his government. Furthermore, he announced a joint project of supplying the schools with computers. In reality, this was not a project yet, as it had simply been mentioned by Jean-Pierre during lunch, when he asked the President if this could be useful for the students. Undoubtedly, he was quick to use this as a political tactic!

The President invited Jean-Pierre and me to join him on stage. He sent one of his bodyguards to find us in the crowd. I had no other choice than to follow him to the improvised platform. It was more than two metres above ground and we reached it by climbing a flight of flimsy stairs. On the platform, the President stood between Jean-Pierre and me and presented us as the benefactors. The crowd applauded and the President awarded us with the official badge of the province. We were escorted back to our place by bodyguards as the President finished his speech.

Then, it was time to proceed to the inauguration of the church. The President stepped down from the platform and was immediately surrounded by a dense crowd, proud to be able to get close to him. All these people headed off toward the front of the church. We stood up and followed them from a distance when all of a sudden the crowd opened up to let a man through who quickly made his way toward me. He took me by the arm and beckoned our group to follow him. I recognized the bodyguard who had pulled us toward the President by pushing through a bunch of parishioners. At that moment, fireworks were set off and cascaded down from the top of the facade of the church to celebrate the inauguration. The fireworks were beautiful, but the hot red ashes were falling all around us. It was clear that local security measures differed considerably from ours!

Whenever the President made a move while visiting the church, he would send his bodyguard to look for us. He really wanted us to be by his side. In his company, we were even given a private tour of the room where the baptismal fonts were located. He took the initiative to explain to us how the circular room had been rebuilt. From there, our whole group followed him outside where he led us up the bell tower of the church. The view from up there was breathtaking and he took the opportunity to be photographed with us on the roof of the church.

After we had been honoured for our visit, as we descended from the roof with the President we were offered a glass of local drink, which was not to my liking, but served with great pride. The President bade us farewell and we boarded our bus after making it a point to shake hands with those who reached out to express their gratitude. This would wrap up this amazing visit with an equally amazing politician.

This would be our last meeting with Vera Ballon. The local people, who had placed so much hope on this man, eager to see the accomplishment of the progress as promised, turned their back on him and had him replaced in the following election. In the meantime, our project would finally have seen the light of day and the Institute would open in March 2005. Unfortunately, some constraints would prevent me from attending the inauguration. In July 2006, I would have the opportunity to visit the *Instituto Agropecuario Valle de Tambo* located at Cocachacra in the Peruvian province of Islay and to see for myself how important this equipment had been to the life of this region.

Finally Some Students!

I must pay tribute to the Yanuhara-Arequipa Rotary Club members who had worked tirelessly for several years in order to set up this Institute. We must realise that accepting this type of challenge was anything but trivial. Furthermore, since the Institute was located more than a two-hour drive from Arequipa, the project, generated by the need to give the young people in this region an opportunity to get a higher education, had overcome all the obstacles in a few months, surprisingly enough for a country where things were sometimes complicated by bureaucracy. This proved once again that the power resulting from the participation of many people and the determination of a small group were able to make the difference.

I must admit that during my visit in 2006, I had been very impressed to see for myself how much of an influence this Institute had on the lives of thousands of people. These young people, who now had the chance to learn new farming techniques without leaving their own region, were proud to stand on the central plaza of the school to listen to the official speeches. For them, a new future had opened up thanks to the work of a handful of people, as many here in America as in Peru. I was proud to have contributed to this achievement.

Thanks to the involvement of the President of the province of Islay, the new buildings were modern and worthy of a Higher Institute. Three pavilions surrounded the central plaza and a room equipped with some twenty new computers allowed the young people to familiarize themselves with this modern tool.

In the rooms where the cooking courses were given, new devices of industrial standard allowed the students to practise their craft with equipment similar to that which they would encounter in the labour market. Industrial bread ovens were also placed at their disposal. During my visit, they had me drink a beverage made of yoghurt and a green fruit from the region known as chirimoya which, although not very pretty, was absolutely delicious.

In order to help the students sell their output and to enable the Institute to be financially self-sufficient, the Mayor of the town of Cocachacra assigned to them a space in the local market. So, on every Saturday, the students could sell their production of yoghurt, bread, cakes, etc.

As I concluded my visit, it was not without pride that I had pictures of me taken in front of the Instituto Superior Tecnologico Valle de Tambo. After five years of efforts, this symbolized the completion of the project which had been and still was very dear to my heart. I received news of the project from time to time over an eight-year period and, to date, more than one hundred and twenty students per year have learned a trade which allows them to earn a better living while studying in their region. I hope that one day I will be able to return to see for myself the overall impact of this project, as I will have played some role in its realization.

3

ECUADOR

Water, Source of Disease or Life?

Standing in the back of a truck travelling on a long beach along the Pacific Ocean reminded me of childhood memories when my father and I went fishing and he would let me sit in the back of our family pick-up truck while driving on forest roads. But here I was in Ecuador, thousands of miles from my home village deep in the forests of northwestern New Brunswick, on the banks of the Pacific Ocean.

This adventure had begun, strangely enough, with a nun visiting my office. One morning, I received a call from Sister Pauline, a nun from the Congregation of the Sisters of Jesus and Mary, who told me she had heard of me and my work at the Rotary from her sister who works with my wife Aline. She insisted on coming to see me at my office, where she arrived a few hours later.

She explained to me that she and other nuns of the Congregation of the Sisters of Jesus and Mary worked in South America. She was seeking funding for the school that the sisters founded in Ecuador. Sister Pauline and Sister Diane, her companion to Cojimies, were also looking for sponsorships for children who wished to attend their school, La Casa de Los Niños. As the parents of this little fishing village were poor, she explained, they could not cover the costs required for school. She also explained that 95% of the children in this village were sick because the water from their well was contaminated. A team of doctors from Colombia had reached this staggering conclusion after examining the children.

To me, this type of sponsorship was more like an individual decision. So I did not see how Rotary, as an organisation, could get involved, especially since our policy is to help groups and communities rather than individuals. Taking care of a water problem is the kind of project that clubs like to achieve in collaboration with the Rotary Foundation of Rotary International. However, these projects can only be achieved with the participation of a local Rotary Club. Therefore, I suggested to Sister Pauline that she contact a club in the Cojimies area which would subsequently submit the project to us.

A few days later, I received a call from Sister Pauline's colleague, Sister Diane Fortier in Ecuador. She explained to me the problem once again. I gave her the name and address of the president of the Rotary Club of Portoviejo San Gregorio located four hours from Cojimies, telling her to contact them to see if they were willing to support this project. I did not want to commit myself at this time because the project seemed quite ambitious. Also, I could not make this decision alone, because it fell within the duties of the governor who would succeed me, my friend Gary Walker.

Although, having very few details, Gary was interested in making this his project of the year for governorship, just as the agricultural institute project had been for my year. In those days, we talked a lot about water projects, since they fall under what is called sustainable development projects. The prospect of realising a project vital to a community appealed as much to me as it did to Gary.

Since I only knew Sister Diane for having spoken to her on the phone, I had no idea this woman could be so determined. Also, shortly after our first contact, I received another phone call from her telling me that she had already contacted the Portoviejo San Gregorio club and they agreed to realise the project. She had made inquiries about the members of this club because according to what she had learned from people of the diocese, the Rotary Clubs of Ecuador were not doing anything good. This bad reputation is probably encouraged by the clergy who would, most likely, desire to receive better support from these clubs. Rotary Clubs, by their charter, are non-religious and apolitical, which does not always please the political and religious authorities. But after looking into the matter, she discovered that the president of the club that year, Dr. Meliton Garcia, had a very good reputation and she felt that she could trust him. She had contacted him to propose her project by saying that in Canada, we were ready to move forward, which was not quite the case.

The first numbers submitted by Sister Diane revolved around $160,000 USD. Given the complexity of the project and the importance of the amount requested, Gary and I decided to go there to check it out ourselves. It is always better to ascertain the situation for ourselves and above all to get to know those with whom we will have to work. Therefore, in March 2003 we left with our wives to visit this small village on the shores of the Pacific. That is how I found myself standing in the back of this pick-up truck travelling on the beach towards Cojimies.

A Village at the End of the World

As Gary left from Maine and I from Quebec, we agreed to rendezvous at the Hilton Colonial hotel in Quito on a Sunday morning in March 2003. A Rotarian of Quito, aware of our visit, gave us a tour around the city and invited us to eat in a *hacienda* where the owners, Fernando and Miriam, manage a restaurant and take care of entertaining clients. She, a beautiful Cuban woman, sings and dances while Fernando accompanies her on the guitar. For our first day in Ecuador, we spent a beautiful afternoon on the outskirts of Quito. Our departure for the coast was planned for the next morning with Sister Diane who organised our transport.

Monday, at six in the morning, Sister Diane joined us at the hotel. She booked two taxis with trusted drivers that often work for the sisters in Quito. We had to leave early to be able to arrive the same day in Cojimies. It was necessary to take advantage of low tide, because the last part of the journey was on the beach.

Sister Diane got into one taxi with Aline and me while Gary and his wife Roberta rode in the other car. We left Quito at 2,743 metres (about 9,000 feet) above sea level to descend to sea level. The scenery was beautiful as we drove through the craggy peaks of the Andes covered with lush vegetation. Although the drivers drove fast, it took more than eight hours to reach the coast. As March is the carnival period, without realising it, we quickly took part in the celebrations and discovered a local custom of this country during this festive period.

Whenever we entered a village, our taxi had to slow down to get over speed bumps installed to reduce the speed of vehicles. In the first village, we were surprised by a group of youths armed with huge water guns and buckets, who took advantage of open windows to soak us while laughing and shouting "Carnival!" Fortunately it was hot outside and our clothes dried quickly! By the second village, as soon as the driver slowed down, we quickly closed the windows to avoid being sprayed. It soon became a race to see who was faster: the one closing the window or the sprayer. This put some animation in our long journey.

Five hours after our departure, we made our first stop to eat in a small town where Sister Diane looked for a restaurant with good hygiene standards. The best that we could find was an American fast food chain which served fried chicken. Although chicken and fries are not a typical meal from this country, at least we are assured that our digestive system will be able to absorb this food without protest. Everyone was happy to stop for a bit to regain their balance after being shaken by our drivers over countless bumps and curves. They knew we were in a hurry to arrive before the end of low tide, because Sister Diane warned them of the importance of arriving on time!

By mid-afternoon, we finally arrived in Pedernales, the capital of the region. It is also the city that our little village Cojimies depends on. As planned, two pick-up trucks driven by villagers were waiting for us in front of the church. We transferred our luggage, including two huge yellow bags of medication for Sister Diane given by Collaboration Santé Internationale which I have already mentioned. We boarded the two pick-up trucks and were on our way to our final destination, Cojimies.

Since the only road to Cojimies is impractical, the best way to get there was via the beach. We therefore left the city by this improvised route. For me this was the most pleasant part of the trip. We drove at over 60 kilometres an hour on the endless beach to cross the 35 kilometres that still separated us from the village. We circumvented a whale that had washed up on shore; a little farther, we needed to slow down to cross a pool of water left by the tide; farther still, we came upon a large tree blocking our way momentarily. Finally, we reached our destination: the Sisters of Jesus-Mary Covent located in the centre of the village.

The sisters' convent was built by the archdiocese and is adjacent to the majestic church whose architecture resembles the hull of a boat. The Sisters, who were expecting visitors, had prepared three small rooms on the ground floor, each with a bathroom and shower. It was modest comfort, but much appreciated. The single beds were a bit hard with their thin foam mattress, no big deal; we had arrived at destination.

After taking a shower and resting for a while, we followed Sister Diane on a tour of the village before sunset. In Ecuador, the sun always sets at the same time, around six o'clock, and gets up at six o'clock in the morning throughout the year. It was during this walk that for the first time, I discovered the slum dwellings on stilts with walls made of planks assembled incorrectly and letting daylight pass through. On the beach, Sister Diane met a woman who was standing near a pile of objects. She talked with her in Spanish for a few minutes then explained that these objects were the entire possessions of the woman and her two grandchildren. The lady explained that the sea had "eaten" her house and the pile of objects was all she had left. The high tide of the day before had eroded the sand and her house had been washed away. The grandmother took care of her two grandchildren while the parents worked abroad.

Having toured the village, we returned to the convent where the sisters offered us dinner. We were in a festive mood as we sat together at the table. We laughed at Aline's fear when she entered the shower: a spider resembling a tarantula was hanging near the top of the wall. Fortunately for her, the little beast had died and dried up on site. She had a good scare. The conversation was lively; we spoke French to each other, English with our friends Gary and Roberta, as well as Spanish with the other two nuns from Colombia who also lived in the convent.

"Alone we go faster, together we go further"

(African proverb)

Sister Diane Takes Charge

We did not waste any time: as of 7 pm, people arrived at the convent to attend the meeting organised by Sister Diane. The sisters set up chairs under the pergola in the centre of the court that is used as a playground for children of the Casa de Niños. All the village officials, the leaders of political parties, as well as the deputy mayor of Pedernales were present. The meeting began with a presentation by Sister Diane on the water situation and the possibility of funding from us. Soon, the interests of various political parties were obvious and openly demonstrated the dissent that existed in the village. Sister Diane quickly interrupted everyone by telling them in an authoritative tone that this was not a political project. She asked party representatives to work for the good of the community and not for their own political interests. After this very clear and unambiguous declaration from our host, the real discussions began. Despite the unanimity created around the project, the deputy mayor did not want to commit himself on behalf of the mayor, who also happened to be his father, who was absent that night for health reasons.

Seeing the hesitation of the deputy mayor, as governor of our Rotary district, I then made him a very clear offer: our Rotary district, in collaboration with the Rotary Foundation, was ready to invest $100,000 USD in the water project on the sole condition that the municipality did the same. Without this contribution from the municipality, we would not invest any money in the project. Gary agreed with me as we confirmed this offer. The deputy mayor said that he could not make that commitment alone, but at least he seemed to support the project. He promised to raise this issue at the next council meeting of Pedernales. The other participants promised to do whatever it took for the project to be approved by the city.

I later learned that it would take a large group of citizens from Cojimies at the council meeting, accompanied by a group from Canada visiting Cojimies which, coincidentally, had brought a camera to film the discussions, to get the municipality to finally agree to approve the project and invest $100,000.

After our second day of visiting the Cojimies area, it was time to leave. Upon leaving the convent, to thank the sisters for their hospitality and their to pay the cost of our stay, I gave Sister Diane a $100 bill. She refused, but I insisted telling her that she would find a way to use the money to help someone. Meanwhile, another Sister arrived. She told Sister Diane she had found a house to relocate the homeless woman and her two grandchildren. She said that she had an agreement with the owner of the house, but she did not know how she would be able to pay the rent of five dollars per month. Sister Diane then showed her the $100 bill and asked if it would be enough. The petite Sister then fell to her knees at my feet, exclaiming that it was the voice of God that spoke. Never has one of my gifts done greater good!

Before leaving Ecuador, Gary and I agreed to visit the Rotary Club of Portoviejo San Gregorio which had volunteered to oversee the project on behalf of Rotary. During the meeting with the club leaders, an engineer brought plans and a cost estimate. What a surprise to learn that the cost of the project amounted to a whopping $360,000! The $100,000 contribution of our district and the Foundation of Rotary International of $100,000 added to that of the municipality amounted to only $200,000! We therefore had to find the missing $160,000. A club member proposed to contact a quasi-governmental organisation called Paraguas that helps Ecuadorian municipalities fund their water projects. A condition of involvement for Paraguas is the financial participation of the villagers. We then suggested considering the Rotary contribution as that of the village, thus satisfying the requirement of the organisation. We then therefore directed that person to take the necessary steps to complete the financing.

Effective Micro-Credit

We left Portoviejo for Guayaquil, the industrial capital of the country, where members of a local Rotary Club were expecting us. Before leaving Canada, doing research on Ecuador, I contacted the Rio Guayas Club whose secretary seemed very active on the

Internet. We were hosted by club members. Aline and I were put up by Gilberto and Teresa who owned a house in a gated community, surrounded by a high cement wall. A guard in his sentry post opened the gate to give us access to the community.

Gilberto owned a very luxurious house. We entered a large hall where you could see a majestic white marble staircase that goes up by turning 90 degrees. Alcoves nestled beautiful sculptures with large framed paintings. Upstairs, each bedroom had its own bathroom, an air conditioning system with remote control and a computer. It was even better than a hotel!

The next morning I could see the cook preparing breakfast for us and a large table that seats at least fourteen guests. When the gardener informed Gilberto that the car was washed and ready, the four of us left to see a micro-credit project funded by a Rotary Club of Maine.

This micro-credit business operated in a very poor neighbourhood with houses made of bamboo like hundreds of thousands of others in Guayaquil. They were manufactured by a non-profit company called Hogar de Cristo, or House of Christ. The small houses were mounted on wooden pillars, allowing the owner to close the space between the pillars with concrete blocks as they gathered money. So, when all four sides were completed, it would give the family another living space on the ground floor.

Micro-credit businesses make an extraordinary contribution to improving the standard of living for its beneficiaries. In this area, the majority of people live on an average of a dollar a day. Their small businesses add about five dollars to this income, which represents a significant improvement in their standard of living. I saw a whole family working to make baskets with strips of plastic, another making candles and a third preparing small bags of spices. All these items were to be sold at the market. We were greeted like royalty! For these people, we were the ones that helped them improve their life. They gave us gifts that we were embarrassed to accept because it would be better for them to sell. But we accepted because it made them so happy to show us their gratitude; we certainly did not want to offend them.

Mr. Minister!

A year later, in 2004, I returned to Ecuador to visit the Portoviejo Club, being the prime contact person for the project. I realised that there were a lot of things left to do in order for everything to materialize. There was no agreement on the choice of construction manager or the contractors. Although my Spanish was deficient, I understood that the local official of the Paraguas organisation had a problem with accepting that the Rotary Club of Portoviejo would be responsible for overseeing the work. After several hours of discussion, we agreed to go to Quito to meet with the Minister of Development (MIDUVI) at his office.

The following Monday, we met at the minister's department. Everybody made the trip: the mayor of Pedernales, citizens of Paraguas, officials from the Portoviejo Club, and Sister Diane who accompanied us. After security formalities, they directed us to the minister's office and invited us to be seated around a large conference table.

From the outset, the Minister told us he was happy to see Rotary International and the Rotary Foundation involved in a project in his country. He added that, being a member of a Rotary Club himself, he looked forward to working with us. The expression on the faces of the Paraguas representatives spoke volumes about their disappointment. Their minister was on our side. Needless to say, it only took a few minutes of discussion to reach an agreement. The project was finally able to come true.

The work was undertaken and Sister Diane kept us regularly informed of what was happening in Ecuador. Members of the Rotary Club of Portoviejo being four hours away from Cojimies, then asked a businessman, Galin Munoz, a resident of Cojimies and also the brother of a Portoviejo Club member, to oversee the work. The villagers also formed a committee for water that was on hand to ensure that the work was well done. One morning, Galin discovered that the main pipe destined to transport water from the wells to the reservoir in the village centre was only four inches in diameter instead of the six inches specified in the plans. Fortunately, Galin realised right away the "error" by the contractor.

Throughout the work, unforeseen delays had hampered construction. It was not until January 2006 that the project was finally completed. Yet again, there were missing water meters needed to connect the last families. The water committee of Cojimies decided to install these meters to ensure that villagers used this water only for human consumption and not for domestic work.

In the summer, upon my return to Cojimies, most homes were connected to the municipal system. They were very proud to have us tour the facilities and they brought my wife Aline and me to the yard of a family so I could see for myself the quality of water and the pressure in the system. Water gushed with force from a small tap installed behind the house. They insisted that Aline and I taste the clean, fresh water for which we had all worked diligently for more than three years.

Usually, I refuse to drink the local water when travelling abroad. It is always risky for a North American living in a sanitized world to drink anything but bottled water. But this time, we could not refuse. I did not want to tell the people of the village that I did not trust the water that I helped bring to them to replace their contaminated wells. Although the quality of the water produced by the wells we dug was highly valued, I still had some fear as I raised the glass to my mouth. The water tasted good and fresh. We drank it without feeling any discomfort afterwards. So, our fragile North-American intestines were able to confirm that the water in Cojimies was really safe.

On a subsequent trip, I had the opportunity to read a study on the water quality in the region. I'm quite proud so say that the water in Cojimies contained less than two parts per million of fecal coliform while samples taken in two restaurants in Pedernales posted over 1,100! Therefore it can be stated that people in Cojimies drink excellent quality water!

Her Again!

A year later, in fall 2007, Sister Diane wrote to inform me that the one and only pump used in the water system was beginning to show signs of fatigue and that a second pump was needed in case the first one failed. More than two hundred families were already connected to the system and requests for new connections continued. If the pump were to fail, the whole system would be paralyzed. I said jokingly that I thought I had finished with her... She laughed at the other end of the line and told me that there would always be ongoing things. Our Rotary District 7790 therefore agreed to fund another pump and applied for a grant from the Rotary Foundation.

Although the water committee managed to collect fees from subscribers, this money was used for the maintenance of the system. A new pump costs about $10,000, which could jeopardize the available capital for several years. But as sponsors of the project, we have a duty to ensure that the system is able to serve the community of Cojimies for many years. So, it is with pleasure that we approved this new application.

Sister Diane also expressed her desire to restore an old reservoir located near the pumping station. The main water line passed a few metres from this reservoir and it would take a small connection under the road to pump the water from there and service another part of the village. Since the cost was not very high, again we decided to go ahead with this new project.

But Sister Diane was not going to stop there! In 2008, she informed us of a problem that had developed with the wells in operation for the past three years. By pumping water out of the well, suction is created at the base of the vertical shafts. This suction draws salt into the water table which is not very deep as the wells are located just half a kilometre from the sea. This gives a slight salty taste to the water in the system, which makes it less pleasant to drink. She therefore requested a new project for the construction of three new wells.

These new wells would also be used to provide water to other areas. In poorer parts of the village, where people settled on land they did not own, a truck supplied their drinking water. These neighborhoods called "invasions" are located on floodplains that nobody wants and no one knows who the owners are. For me it was important that these people also have quality drinking water.

The following year, during a visit to Ecuador to follow up on another project we were sponsoring in the Guayaquil area, I returned to Cojimies to see how the project for the new tank and new pump was progressing. Walking through the village, I saw that some neighbours shared their water by connecting two families on the same pipe. This allowed them to split the bill in two, depriving the village committee of revenue for the maintenance of the system. For a moment, I was a little shocked by this discovery. But after all, our project was designed to bring safe drinking water to as many people as possible. Sharing the water with their neighbours contributed to this goal. So, even though this approach deprived the water committee of income, it was not up to me but up to the committee to collect the money owed.

Yet Another Project...

As our projects in Cojimies drew to a close, or so I thought, in 2008, the committee of international action in our district prepared to launch a tender to fund a large-scale project financed over three years. We realised with the project in Cojimies that by getting involved with a village over a longer period of time, we had a greater impact and our actions met the definition of sustainable development more effectively.

Therefore, we set out to define a series of criteria which represented our objectives and we then sent our tender to several Rotarians we know in South America. One of my friends from Argentina, who wanted to help us, conveyed the offer to several clubs in South America. As a result we were flooded with proposals. A total of thirty-four projects were submitted!

Only a dozen projects met our criteria. We then realised that the people of these countries had difficulty imagining being able to achieve large-scale projects. We were talking about $300,000 US over three years. None of the projects received reached that amount. The seven members of the committee made an initial list of the five projects they preferred. From there, we established a new list of five projects which received the most votes. During the committee meeting, we arrived at two finalists and, for logistical reasons, the new project from Sister Diane was retained!

She was the only one to have met all the conditions of the tender. In addition, we were confident that the project would succeed and would be well supervised. Her project was to add a filtration system and chlorination to the existing system as well as new wells in the districts of Churo and Aguacate. These were located five kilometres from the village centre and therefore could not be connected to the existing system. Moreover, as they were on higher ground, it was not certain that the current system of pumps had the capability of pushing the water to them.

One of our conditions had been that our Rotarians in the district would have the opportunity to visit the project site and that we would possibly to do a bit of the work ourselves. In March 2010, I accompanied the first group of fifteen people mostly from the State of Maine, part of which belonged to our Rotary district. Governor Sylvia Plourde from Maine, who had agreed to support the project, accompanied us with her son. My daughter Isabelle also joined the group.

Peter Garrett of Waterville was included in the trip. Peter is a hydrologist. I had the opportunity to tell him about the problems of salinity in the water. He had a solution for this common problem for wells located close to the sea. So, I scheduled a meeting with him, the two municipal councillors and the village water committee.

Peter's idea was to dig horizontal wells instead of vertical wells. He explained in technical details how the wells operated. Instead of digging deep, the idea was to dig long trenches at the bottom of which a manifold was installed to bring the water to a tank where it could be pumped. No suction, therefore no salt in the water. Simple solution when you think of it. Peter is a very competent man who has worked on such wells in England as well as in some Caribbean islands.

The people from Cojimies attending the meeting listened to Peter but were skeptical. The meeting ended after three hours without anyone being convinced. We then agreed, before embarking on such a venture, that research would have to be done to find out if the specialized equipment needed to drill such wells was available in Ecuador.

The project began during my trip with a second group of people in the fall of 2010. The filtration equipment was installed, the land was fenced in and the opening of a vertical well was completed. The project engineer, Julio Rodrigues, decided to try the horizontal-well technique in another area near the pumping station. Unfortunately, this first horizontal well was not completed at the time of our visit; it was too early to know the results.

It was not until the following year, in December 2011, that I returned to Cojimies. The work was finished by then and they wanted to organise an official ceremony as part of the village's centennial celebrations. Claude Martel, who succeeded Governor Sylvia, joined me for this trip. They brought us to Aguacate and Churo for the official opening. What a surprise to be told by Julio, the engineer that these villages were now being served by horizontal wells instead of the vertical wells that had originally been planned! Unable to find the groundwater that is needed to drill a vertical well, he tried the technique suggested by our colleague Peter Garrett. This resulted in producing plenty of water which was of high quality. For Claude, it was an emotional moment when he saw water gush out of the new system in Churo and Aguacate. Local residents had organised a party to celebrate this milestone in the life of their community.

In late afternoon, the village authorities accompanied by the water committee of Cojimies had held a ceremony to celebrate the end of the work. Claude and I were given large plaques of appreciation and souvenir gifts for all the work done in their community. I then had the opportunity to speak and thank them for their commitment to their community and to encourage them to continue working for their village. My little speech to the village authorities would undoubtedly be my last official activity in Cojimies. Having accomplished that which brought us to Cojimies in 2003, it was now time to continue our work elsewhere.

The day ended with the closing ceremony of the village centennial celebrations. They wanted to thank me by asking me to act as a judge for the selection of Miss Cojimies 2011, but I politely refused and I was content to attend the party with Sister Diane and Claude. That evening in my little room at the convent I could hear the echoes of the disco music of the festival. I could not help but think of all the progress made since my first visit. For me, it was mission accomplished!

Water, a Spark Plug

During all these years, I have seen how the village had developed. I realise, in hindsight, that the water project had created an important awareness among residents of Cojimies. Used to being left behind, those who lived isolated at the end of their small peninsula had managed to convince the authorities of Pedernales to subsidize their water project. This made them realise that by working together they could influence the authorities.

The many political parties of the country battled not only nationally, but also at the municipal level. This created never-ending disputes which only contributed to dragging things out. After their confrontation with the city council to raise money for water, residents of Cojimies decided to undertake another battle of equal importance. They wanted a drivable road between Pedernales and their village located thirty-five kilometres away.

This awareness of teamwork for the good of the community is the main reason why today there is a beautiful new road between Pedernales and Cojimies. No need to travel along the beach. Every morning a bus now takes villagers to their workplace in Pedernales.

Travel by the beach was perhaps more scenic, but when an emergency occurred, they had to hope for low tide.

The new road also brought economic development. Today, new hotels and restaurants have sprung up to accommodate tourists. Large posters advertise beaches in Cojimies. They started to develop the waterfront to install small shops like any self-respecting tourist spot! I like to think that our participation in the water project was the spark plug for the revival of this village.

During a conversation with Sister Diane on my last trip in 2011, she told me that things were not moving fast enough. For her, there was still so much to do... But for me, visiting only once a year, I am better suited to see that things are improving. After water and the road, the school had been renovated and a new wing had been added, which eliminated the small private schools which were dilapidated and often unsafe buildings.

Other projects that the people of Rotary International completed in Cojimies include computers that allow young people to be in touch with this technology despite their poverty. There is also the school yard in cement, the "cancha" which allows children to stay dry during the rainy season, the roof of another school that we helped to pay for and ultimately the equipment we provided for the small health centre. In the latter case, it allows the weekly presence of a nurse who meets with patients and administers examinations, so they no longer have to travel to Pedernales.

Of course, all these changes occurred over more than a decade. When you live in that kind of environment, I can understand that you think it's not going fast enough. But the transformation that has taken place in this village has also brought a lot of inconveniences such as an increasing number of cars, honking from buses that go around the village twice every morning around six o'clock to let people know that it's almost time to leave for work. So it would seem that progress brings with it some negative elements. Quiet times are now long gone!

We Are Not Poor ... We Are Less Than That!

In 2004, we agreed to support a project near the town of Salinas in the Santa Helena Peninsula, a two-hour drive from Guayaquil, Ecuador. The Governor at the time, Elaine Toussaint, chose this project for her governorship year. Rotarians from the Rio Guayas Guayaquil Rotary Club wanted to teach agriculture to the people of this region to reduce the influx of newcomers seeking employment in the city. They were considering creating community gardens for fishermen's wives in order to increase their family income.

A series of problems, such as the lack of water and lack of interest from fishermen for agriculture, prevented the project from being realised in its original form. In collaboration with the Coastline Polytechnic School, Espol (Escuela Politecnica Del Litoral), they opted instead to develop a hands-on course to teach people in the area, who already did a little gardening, some modern techniques such as culture beneath a tunnel, drip irrigation, etc. Thus was born Agrofuturo, a training and agricultural production centre.

The promoters of the project, Rotarians and Espol, acquired a large lot so that students could immediately apply what they learned. They could connect to the Grand Canal which brings water to the region. On the lot they also built a shelter that served as a classroom with toilets.

Classes are given in thirteen-week sessions. In order to study, students must promise to return to their villages and teach others what they have learned. In the beginning, students had to travel daily from their village to the training site. Later, a dormitory was built to allow them to stay there during the week.

I had the opportunity to visit the training centre on at least four occasions. Each time, I was amazed to see teachers from Espol in the middle of the field wearing work overalls and rubber boots, teaching young people the different techniques. Here, there were no closed classrooms in large buildings, only a shelter to hide from the sun when it was time for theoretical training. This direct involvement of teachers has always impressed me. Maybe it's because I do not visit the experimental farms of our universities.

The courses really achieved good results. In this arid region, growing watermelons using traditional methods yields about one ton per acre. With the techniques taught at Agrofuturo, yields were ten times greater, or more than ten tons per acre! Imagine the difference for someone who has a small piece of land to grow food for his family!

In December 2011, I went to Agrofuturo to show this project to Claude Martel, governor in 2010-2011, who had already developed his own District project in Ecuador. That day was a recruiting day for the next session. Under the shelter, about thirty people were waiting: candidates and parents who accompanied their children.

After receiving explanations from teachers concerning the courses, there was time for questions. A lady got up and addressed the professor with these words: "Sir, I beg you, take at least one student from our village. We desperately need to improve our situation. In our village, we are not poor ... we are less than that! Our houses are not houses; they are just a bunch of planks and bits of metal. I beseech you, sir, accept one of our youth so that they may learn! "

It was truly a cry from the heart that touched me deeply. This woman knew that if a candidate was chosen from her village, he would show others what he had learned. She believed that it was the only way for them to improve their lives and attenuate their misery. As I write this, I can still see this woman begging the teacher. I felt the distress in her voice... No one could remain indifferent to her request. Rarely had human misery been expressed so clearly in so few words.

The Agrofuturo project has been very successful. Discussions with Japanese people are underway to fund another such centre in the region. Showing people how to feed themselves rather than feeding them: that's what this training centre will have achieved.

4

THE AFRICAN EXPERIENCE

A Child Will Die

In 2003 I was invited to join a group of Rotarians from the Toronto area who had organised a trip to participate in a National Polio Immunization Day in Cameroon. Since Rotary International has given itself the mission to help eradicate polio, this was a golden opportunity to participate in this ambitious project. Rotary has partnered with the World Health Organization (WHO), UNICEF and the Centre for Disease Control in Atlanta to put an end to this terrible disease. The effort of Rotarians is primarily financial, but in the countries affected by polio, Rotarians are actively involved in immunization. Thus, at major vaccination campaigns called National Immunization Days (NIDs), Rotarians from around the world support local Rotarians. I had never had the opportunity to go to Africa before, so I jumped in and joined the group of about thirty-five people: our destination was Douala, an industrial city located on the coast in Cameroon.

The group met for the first time at Charles de Gaulle airport in Paris. Members had agreed to meet there given the fact they came from the United States, Australia, Canada (mostly from the Toronto area, and a few including myself from Quebec). All of us had heard of these trips that were organised every year by Barry Howie and his wife Jane. Participants are motivated not only by a desire to participate in NIDs, but also by the desire to see Africa. Some had already participated in one or two other trips before, but most of us were at our first African experience.

When you arrive in Africa for the first time, it's a real shock. As soon as we left the Douala airport, the overwhelming heat and humidity overcame us. For those of us who were arriving from Canada at the end of February, the temperature difference was huge. We were greeted by Rotarian Bawa Mankoube, Vice President of the polio campaign in Africa. Since we were considered humanitarian workers, the formalities of customs and immigration were quickly resolved. Indeed, after the basic formality of stamping our passports, we soon found ourselves on the sidewalk where our guide led us to a bus that was waiting for us. A compact crowd of vendors of all kinds pressed against the gates of the airport offering passengers either souvenirs or cheap taxis or simply offering to carry our bags. The group organiser had already hired baggage handlers to load part of our luggage in the back of the bus and the rest on the roof. I tried to keep an eye on my bag because, with all these people around, I was a little worried. We found ourselves in a totally different world than the one to which we were accustomed. Everything had been done in an indescribable mess. With the humidity, the heat and all these people around us, I must admit that I was glad to get on the bus. Vendors kept chasing us as we left the terminal. Even as we sat in the bus, they knocked on the windows in an attempt to sell us their goods. Soon, we were headed for the Akva Palace Hotel where we would be staying during our trip.

Before I left Canada, a Rotarian friend of French origin, Georges Mosser, who had worked as an engineer in the construction of the hotel, told me that right after the hotel had opened its doors and before security measures had been installed, prostitutes would roam the corridors and knock on bedroom doors muttering: "Boss, boss, love is here"! So he told me, "If love knocks, let it pass!"

With this advice in mind, I spent my first night in Africa. Tired as I was, I slept well, but a member of our group who suffered from insomnia due to jet lag, had decided to walk around the hotel. He told me that as he arrived in the lobby, a group of prostitutes began knocking on the windows when they saw him. The situation had not changed much since my friend George had worked there several years ago.

The next morning, we were up at six o'clock and after breakfast the group met at seven o'clock in the hotel lobby. We were all eager to begin the first day of vaccination. We piled into two minibuses offering rudimentary comfort. We were four in a row, two on the double seat, one on a single seat and the fourth in the jump seat. This made it possible to transport eighteen people in these minibuses no larger than a regular minivan. We were not used to travelling this way, but our good mood won over and we quickly learned to love our neighbour! We thus travelled for more than an hour on a dirt road, which is so characteristic of West Africa, before arriving in a village that was expecting us.

For this first day, we were taken to a remote village outside Douala where all the locals had gathered for the occasion. For this village, it was a celebration: the authorities from the Ministry of Health were present and the villagers put on their traditional costume. Like good tourists, once out of our minibus, we began taking photos. We were now in the heart of Africa. To begin, we had to greet the village elders who were lined up in the shade under a Baobab tree. We stopped for a moment to take a few photos and then marched one after the other in front of the elders who were happy to greet us. Unlike what happens in North America, elders still have their place and play an important role in African life. To not salute the elders would have been disrespectful.

The place was huge: to one side, the students dressed in costumes were lined up quietly in front of the school with their teacher standing beside them. I was impressed by their silence and calmness. In front of them, on the other side of the square, the dancers dressed in their traditional costumes, waited for a sign. Then, not too far away, stood the villagers observing the scene.

After the welcoming speeches were over and done with, acknowledgments were made on our behalf by our group leader, Barry, and then the dancers started their performance. At the sound of drums, they danced in the middle of the square. When their feet hit the ground forcefully a red cloud of dust would rise. For me, the scene was almost surreal with the drums echoing in my head. I closed my eyes for a moment and just listened. Next I thought to myself: Hey I am actually in Africa!

But there was a lot of work ahead. So, right after the dancing had ended, we got down to the task at hand. They gave us vaccine vials that were to be administered to children under five. As the Sabin vaccine was an oral vaccine, all we had to do was simply deposit two drops in the mouth of the child who would then be protected against polio. Since there were many of us, we went quickly through the rows of children and the work was soon completed. The day unfolded in this manner and we went from village to village. When we returned to the hotel in the evening around seven o'clock, we were glad the day was over. Our breakfast was long gone and a good meal was greatly appreciated.

The Islands of Douala

The next morning, I volunteered to go to the islands of Douala in the Estuary of the Ouri River. I left with a Rotarian from Douala who drove us in his own car to the port where we had to take a boat. When we arrived at the port, a large crowd of people had already gathered there despite the early hour. Our group followed the guide in single file through the fish market so that we could get to our boat. Crossing the market was quite an experience in itself. The morning heat and humidity added to the smell of fish and sweat gave the place a unique character. The alley was packed with vendors' stalls on each side. As the crowd was moving quickly in the narrow path, we had to push and shove our way through to continue following our guide. I could sense the many astonished faces as I made my way through. I say on "my way", because I felt very alone in this place even through it did not appear hostile to me. It struck me that very few white people would dare to venture into these areas. For the first time, I felt like I was part of a visible minority. It was a very strange feeling, one that I was not used to and I did not feel very comfortable being there.

While I was sitting in the boat waiting to leave, I observed the following scene: Fishermen were cleaning their fish before going to sell it at the market and they were calling out to each other as they did so. They were watching us and seemed quite intrigued to see a dozen or so white people invade their world. Our captain had to deal with some minor mechanical problems and after several minutes of waiting, we headed out to sea. Our boat was equipped with a powerful engine that moved rapidly in the channels between the islands. I sensed that if we were to be pursued by bandits we would not be able to go any faster! Our captain obviously enjoyed showing off his speedboat and he tried to impress us by navigating the banks of the channels with the engines at full throttle.

We stopped at an island with a few fishermen's huts. As prescribed by local customs, we had to introduce ourselves to the chief, so, after landing, we set off along a path that led to the centre of the island. After ten minutes of walking, we noticed the chief's house. In reality, he was an official of the government of Cameroon. He lived in a cement house and although it was nearly ten o'clock in the morning, we found him still in bed. Personally, I found it very strange to find a government official in bed at this time of day... but then again, other countries other customs, I told myself.

He invited us in and offered us to take a seat in a room that would be considered his living room where he usually greeted islanders who wanted to see him. After a brief exchange of courtesies, we explained the purpose of our visit. After obtaining his consent, we returned to the boat to set off for the other islands where we would finally begin our vaccination work. Upon our arrival on a larger and more populated island, we headed to the school where a group of cheerful and smiling children were waiting for us. Fairly quickly after the initial rush had subsided, everyone was vaccinated. Some of my colleagues in their haste to participate in the program even resorted to a little pushing and shoving in order to immunize the greatest possible number of children. I observed the scene from the outskirts and was happy to be able to take pictures of the smiles of children who were intrigued by the visit of a group of white people.

To avoid wasting vaccines, we had to be careful not to vaccinate children over five years old, given that the risk of contracting polio was minimal for them. To determine if a child was less than five years old, we used the following technique: we would ask the children to touch their left ear by passing their right hand over their head or vice versa. Children who were able to reach their ear with their opposite arm were considered to be more than five years old. To recognize those who had been vaccinated, we applied dark nail polish on the nail of their little finger. This way, we would avoid administering a double dose of vaccine to a child, which could be dangerous since the Sabin vaccine is a live vaccine.

The vaccine also had to be stored in a cold environment, what we called the cold chain. In a country as hot as Cameroon, this was quite a problem. We had to carry vials of vaccine in small coolers. The vials were equipped with a sensor that would change colour when heated, which allowed us to know if the bottle we were about to open was still good. This cold chain required constant monitoring in the distribution of the vaccine. This increased the cost of distribution especially since the regions where the vaccine was needed were often in remote locations like the islands in the Estuary of the Ouri River. After completing the vaccination at the school, we stopped at the infirmary of the island. This is where I was to experience the most difficult moments of this journey.

The infirmary was a wooden hut on stilts. As we entered, a few people were waiting to meet the nurse. Our arrival disturbed their tranquility, but people still greeted us with a smile.

Cameroon has eight French speaking provinces and two English speaking ones. The islands where the vaccinations were taking place were English speaking. However, the only nurse on the island was a francophone. Since I was the only francophone in our group he took me aside and invited me to follow him to a treatment room where a mother and a child of about four years old were waiting. Upon entering the small room, I was struck by the lack of privacy and confidentiality. The walls were made of ill-fitting planks through which we could see the light of day coming from outside. Moreover, there was no glass in the window and everyone could hear what was being said between the patient and the nurse.

The nurse explained that the child was suffering from a common childhood disease in this region and needed antibiotics to get better. To keep antibiotics, you need a refrigerator, but there was no electricity on the island. He then showed me the only medication locker that was at his disposal. This cabinet was less than a metre wide and a metre and half in height and it was barely half full. He explained that without proper care the child would soon die. He desperately needed antibiotics.

I suggested to the nurse to let us take the child with us when we went back to Douala in the evening, so that we could take him to the hospital. The nurse translated my offer to the mother in the local dialect. The mother looked at me and seemed terrified. To allow her child to go to Douala was like giving her child to a stranger and risk losing it forever. Seeing the embarrassment and pain of this poor woman, I quickly explained to the nurse that she did not have to decide on the spot, because we had to come back to the island later that afternoon before returning to Douala. We needed to come back to get our friends who had stayed behind to complete the vaccination. Meanwhile, my team and I had to go vaccinate on other islands, so the mother had all day to make this important decision. The nurse translated my offer and I left the room overwhelmed by what I had just experienced.

The White Man Will Come...

We returned to the boat and headed out to the neighbouring islands. I was accompanied by a local nurse who knew the islands as well as my colleague Peter Smith from Halifax. A few minutes after taking off, our captain noticed a canoe of fishermen in the distance. Suspecting there may be children on board, the captain made a ninety degree turn and headed for the small boat. Indeed, a young child of about two years old was on board. The nurse explained the reason of our presence to the father and he agreed to have his child vaccinated. Peter took care in giving the precious drops of vaccine to the child whose mouth was already full of rice. The child did not appreciate the experience and let us know with a few tears. We then left for another island.

The captain slowed the boat as we approached the island. There was no wharf, so we headed for the beach. As soon as we hit bottom, Peter and I were about to take off our shoes to jump in the few centimetres of water between us and the shore. The nurse explained that it would be better for us not to get out, because the black and muddy ground contained parasites that might seep into our skin and make us sick. So, Peter and I agreed to stay in the boat while the captain and the nurse went to vaccinate the few children who lived in the village. We took the opportunity to drink some water as the sun was intense and the heat and humidity overwhelmed us.

On the next island, the vaccination ran smoothly and without incident. Things continued this way as we sailed from island to island throughout the day. On a particular island, we dropped our anchor near a huge tree trunk that served as wharf. We disembarked while trying to keep our balance on this slippery trunk which was covered with moisture. We then went to the chief's house who welcomed us. After the usual explanations, he rang the bell to gather up the children of the village. Peter and I prepared the vaccines while the nurse took care of the control sheets that had to be filled out for each immunization session.

Children started to line up as Peter was preparing to begin the vaccination. As soon as Peter approached the first child, he started screaming. He managed to drop the two precious drops of vaccine into his mouth despite the toddler crying heartbreakingly. The second child cried just as much and so did every child afterwards. I took Peter's place, but I wasn't able to do any better. Every child we approached started screaming. We therefore asked the nurse to take over and she was able to vaccinate all the remaining children without a peep. As she vaccinated the children one by one, she glanced over to us and smiled.

After returning to the boat, Peter and I wondered what we had done to make the children cry so much. The nurse explained that on this island, when children disobeyed their parents, they were told that if they did not listen the "white man would come." These poor children had never seen white people before and here there were two of us trying to put something in their mouth. They were obviously terrified by the sight of these "boogeymen" that their parents had warned them about! Upon hearing this explanation, I realised once again that I was a stranger in this country and that I was the one who was different. And this difference could be very scary, especially for children.

At the end of the day, we returned to the first island to pick up our friends. Everyone was on the beach. While the fishermen repaired their nets, the cheering crowds had been waiting for our arrival with our colleagues. Children quickly surrounded us and looked at us with great curiosity while offering us their best smiles. Upon landing, I looked for the nurse who had to give me the answer from the mother regarding her sick child. There he was, our eyes meet and he signaled no with his head. The mother decided to keep her child with her ... I had to accept her decision even though it made me sad.

For us Westerners, this decision may seem incomprehensible, but after reflection I realised that for the mother, the decision created more uncertainty than the disease itself. This woman had probably never been to a big city. She probably had no money to pay the doctor, to spend the night and even return to her island. To entrust her child with us and remain on her island was equally unacceptable because there was no way of knowing whether she was ever going to see her child again. For us, this decision seemed easy, but for this woman it was very different. Still, I cannot blame her for making this decision, because for her, the death of her child was part of life, her life.

While in the boat that took us back to Douala, I couldn't help but think about this woman and her child. The pain that I had seen in her eyes kept coming back to me. I even regret having made the suggestion to bring the child to Douala. Should I have consulted with the nurse first?

Back at the hotel, we talked things over to see if we could find a solution for the lack of medication and electricity on this island. The situation threatened the lives of children and probably that of other people as well. What could we do to? Various options were discussed and each time we realised the difficulties that had to be overcome if we wanted to help. Install a generator? Who would pay for gasoline? How would the fuel be transported to the island? Solar power? Why not, in a country with so much sun!

But who could repair the unit if it were to break down? The people were not educated, making this option impractical and hardly viable. A problem that may appear quite easy to solve at home became almost insurmountable over here. The lack of financial resources and the lack of training are other factors with which we had to deal with constantly.

Recently I had the opportunity to meet my old travelling companion, Peter Smith from Halifax. He returned several times to Cameroon since that first vaccination trip. He also shipped several containers of medical equipment. He made sure that the small clinic on the island received a new delivery table and hospital beds. Unfortunately, there is still no electricity on the island, so antibiotics are still not available.

As is often the case in this kind of mission, that day we didn't have time to stop and eat lunch. Obviously, on these poor islands, there are no restaurants and certainly no McDonald's! So, once back at the hotel it was with great joy back that the whole group gathered at the pizzeria across the street, boulevard de la Liberté. Together that evening, we appreciated our privileged situation. Nobody lingered, because the day had been rather challenging. The other part of the group which had not gone to the islands ended up in a village where the inhabitants had to install elevated boardwalks over wetlands. Of rudimentary design, these rickety walkways were perched a few metres above the ground and some of the participants found it difficult to negotiate them. Walking on these tall, narrow sidewalks even made some of them dizzy. After only two days, a few members of the group were already beginning to feel the fatigue. This was going to be a long week.

Not Used to Seeing White People Here!

On the third day, the group met again in the hotel lobby to wait for the minibus. We were first led to a clinic located just outside Douala from where all the teams would then depart for their respective vaccination areas. As I was waiting, I heard Barry, our group leader request a replacement for a woman on the team who wanted to change her area of assignment because she did not want to have to take a boat. I volunteered, which meant that I would be paired with Allan, a dentist from the Toronto area.

When our driver arrived, the nurse who was to accompany us sat down in front with the driver, so Allan and I sat in back. A few blocks from the clinic, our car embarked on a dirt road along a coconut plantation. After a while, palm trees were replaced by banana trees. Banana bunches were wrapped in blue plastic to keep insects away. We drove at least twenty minutes before the car came to a stop in a clearing at the edge of a river. The nurse explained that a dugout canoe would pick us up so that we could continue our journey to the other side. After about ten minutes of waiting, a long canoe arrived. We boarded this rudimentary boat driven by a man clearly accustomed to manoeuvring the long, narrow watercraft. This was my dugout canoe baptism. Since first reading about it, this type of canoe has always seemed mythical to me, maybe because of its primitive nature or the fact that it is built right into a tree trunk! Whatever the case, I climbed into the canoe as happy as if I had entered the space shuttle. We took off for a three-minute journey, just long enough to take some pictures before arriving on the other side.

From there, the nurse showed us the path. She was very familiar with the road because she had been assigned by the clinic to oversee the health of the people in this village. Along the way, she showed us the different kinds of trees and explained why white plastic bottles were hanging on palm trees. These bottles were placed there to collect sap for making wine, a bit like the way we reap the sap of maple trees to make maple syrup. What struck me most were the dirty bottles. I was thinking to myself that this wine was most likely not made in the best hygienic conditions. After ten minutes of walking in more than 40° heat, soaked in sweat, we finally saw the first village huts.

We were soon walking toward the centre of the village to meet the chief. He was in the centre of the square, sitting in the shade doing some braiding under a straw-roofed shelter with open sides. He invited us to sit with him while the nurse explained the purpose of our visit. He had already been informed of our visit some time ago and he had no objections. While we were talking things over with the chief, three young men of high stature arrived. Their biceps were bigger than my thighs and and their chest muscles remind me of weightlifters. This left no doubt as to the nature of their work. They were plantation workers and they surely had to exert great physical effort every day to have developed this kind of imposing musculature. They did not bother to greet us and one of them said: "We're not used to seeing white people here..."

I said to myself, "It's time to think fast!" I cast a glance toward my partner Allan and I realised that he has a fair complexion just like me and skin as white as mine. So I turned to the young man who just spoke, "You are really lucky! Real white folks have been sent to you! "

While saying this, I lifted the lower part of my pants to show him my very white legs. I then showed him my arms that were also as equally very pale. He looked at me, looked at his partner and then burst into laughter. My reply, which surprised him, seemed satisfactory as he then offered me some palm wine. After seeing the dirty plastic bottles they used to collect the sap, I politely declined saying that I did not drink wine. This was a lie, but I really did not want to get sick from drinking this palm wine. He then offered me a beer which I accepted with pleasure. We were told that the beer was manufactured under license with hygienic conditions according to European standards, and that it was not dangerous to our fragile North American digestive system. Since it was particularly hot that day, the prospect of drinking a cold beer made me happy. So I accepted his beer and so did Allan. Unfortunately, the beer was not cold. I should have known. They probably did not have electricity. Nevertheless, it was not too warm and it managed to quench my thirst.

While we were drinking our beer, the young men picked up the chief's bell and went around the village to gather the children.

Quickly, a line formed and we were able to administer the vaccines. Within fifteen minutes all the children had been vaccinated except for a two-week-old baby left which we had to vaccinate in his mother's hut. At least this one would not get polio. It was then time to leave. We returned to the river along the same path that had brought us to the village. The canoe was waiting for us and we quickly arrived on the other side.

As is often the case in Africa, our driver had not yet arrived even though we were on time. On site there was a taxi that was so old that it could not be registered to go on the main road. It was a rusty 1981 Toyota Corolla. The car was already 22 years old! There were four men busy loading the trunk with big boxes. The engine hood was open. Since our taxi had not yet arrived, our attendant decided to ask the driver if he could bring us back. She came back a few minutes later and told us that we could take this one instead. Neither Allan nor I objected.

Upon leaving, I saw the driver put the gas supply pipe in his mouth to raise the gas to the carburetor. Then he ran to take a seat in the car while the other three men pushed to start the car. After some hesitation, convulsions and coughing from the engine, the car finally started. The driver waved us to board.

What a surprise to see the other four men who were present board the car along with the three of us! How did we manage to fit seven adults in a small Toyota? It's simple: three men in the front seat, Allan, the nurse and I packed in the back seat and the seventh sitting on the roof! With its cramped group of passengers, the cab drove off on the dirt road to reach the main road.

The heat was unbearable. We rolled the windows down to get a little breeze. Here we were three grown adults packed side by side, but it could have been worse. Fortunately, we only had a half-hour drive, and that was fine. Off we went with three people sitting in the front, three in the back, one man sitting on the roof and the trunk wide open overflowing with boxes.

From our very first pothole we felt the shocks hitting hard. The weight of all these beautiful people, in addition to the trunk, was way too much for the shock absorbers that had probably already been abused quite a bit. Immediately after the first "bong" from the shock absorbers, the roof made a cracking sound under the weight of the passenger. At every pothole we heard the bong from the shock absorbers, followed by a crack. Bong, crack, bong, crack! Allan and I looked at each other and laughed at the situation. Things got even more complicated once we reached the banana plantation. The sprinkler system had been activated and the rotating heads of the system splashed us quite thoroughly! Every ten metres, we got a stream of water right in the face.

Bong, crack, splash!

Bong, crack, splash!

Being loaded down the way we were, we felt each and every pothole on the road. We closed the windows of the car to avoid being continuously sprayed. I was thinking about our friend on the roof, as he could not avoid anything. He also had to try to hold on to the thin edge of the roof which could not have been an easy task! We drove a good ten minutes and the heat inside the car became absolutely suffocating. As soon as we tried to roll the windows down, the water hit our faces as if we were in our shower. This was an absolutely incredible situation. Nobody would ever believe this unimaginable story!

We finally met the taxi that was supposed to pick us up. The nurse who had seen him coming asked our driver to stop so we could change cars. Allan and I were relieved and I guess our traveling companions must have been as well! We returned to the clinic that night with our heads full of anecdotes. Every time I looked at Allan, we couldn't stop laughing. When people asked us what was so funny we told them that we could not tell them because they would not believe us anyway. I thanked the lady who refused to go on the boat that morning for allowing me to live this adventure that will stay with me as one of my most memorable souvenirs.

The next day, we were back in the lobby again which had now become a ritual. We gobbled up our breakfast and went back to our room to grab our backpacks before regrouping once again for the day ahead. This was only our fourth day and already some group members were very tired and decided to stay at the hotel. Personally, although I found the days long, the idea of staying at the hotel did not even cross my mind. I was starting to feel tired, but I wanted to experience this adventure all the way. Since this was our last day of vaccination, I wanted to make the most of it right to the end.

New day, new clinic. This time we were vaccinating children living in an isolated area of the city, a neighbourhood of fishermen on the coast. We created new teams of two with a local worker and off we went. Each team was assigned a few streets to cover. That day, two families refused the vaccines for their children. We tried to explain the benefits of the vaccine to one father, but he would not listen. We did not insist. We simply sat back while the mothers of other children in the neighbourhood pressured the reluctant father. They were afraid that an unvaccinated child would contaminate newborns before the next vaccination was to take place. The pressure from the core worked. Someone summoned us to return to vaccinate the children whose parents had refused the vaccination a few minutes earlier. It was with pleasure that we went back and once these children had been vaccinated, we continued on our journey. The heat was absolutely stifling. I only sweat on rare occasions, but here I felt like my t-shirt was soaked. I must admit that the week had started to take its toll on me. The heat was becoming more and more of a nuisance, especially since I was not used to long walks at over 45 degrees. It is hard to believe that only a few days ago, I was in Quebec in winter temperatures of -20°. I must admit that this was quite a change! Luckily, we only had a few houses left to visit and our day would be done.

We were the first to arrive at the clinic. As soon as we sat in the shade, I noticed a refreshment stand on the other side of the street. At the mere thought of drinking a cold beer, I found enough energy to get up and ask my companions to follow me. This round was on me! When I told the bartender that I was paying for my friends, he looked me and said, "What about me? Aren't you not going to buy me a drink?"

Rather than argue with him, I told him to take one for himself too. The three beers in addition to the one for the server cost me less than one beer at a bar at home. Still it was the first time I had ever heard a server asking clients to offer him a drink. Other countries, other customs! Never had a beer been so appreciated.

A Frustrated Queen!

As the vaccination was now completed, we had the next day off. Local organisers proposed that we drive inland up to Bamenda. Up to that point we had not seen much of Cameroon except for the areas where we went to vaccinate. Everyone accepted this idea, especially since it was only a four-hour drive away.

We had to bring our luggage for the trip to Bamenda. The drivers loaded it onto the roofs of the minibuses. So, in addition to having to support the weight of at least seventeen people, these vehicles also had to bear the weight of all our suitcases. We piled into the two overloaded minibuses and set off for Bamenda. On our way there, as soon as we left the city, we had to stop roughly every five kilometres for road checks. Sometimes it was for customs, sometimes it was the police and each time the driver had to show his papers. According to our guide, Bawa, the reason for these road checks was the possible presence of rebels. Fortunately, our minibus was clearly identified with the logo of Rotary International and the polio vaccination. This helped us to go faster and in some cases we were waved through without having to stop. We were packed like sardines and as we say amongst ourselves, you had better learn to love your neighbour and quick. The atmosphere remained cheerful despite the accumulated fatigue from the week.

After more than two and a half hours, we stopped at the summer home belonging to one of the local Rotarians who wished to meet us. The minibus turned onto a small road that led to a property surrounded by a concrete wall over two metres high. Once past the gates, we could see the house a few hundred metres away perched on a small hill. Everyone was happy to finally stretch their legs and go to the bathroom.

Seeing us arrive, the servants were busy hustling around to garnish the large table set up outside. They brought refreshing juice and drinks for us. Several fellow members from the same Rotary Club as our host were also present and all these beautiful people were walking in the garden and enjoying the unique view and fresh air. After an hour and a half of pleasantries, we went back to our minibus and continued our trip to Bamenda.

The numerous road blocks and poor quality of the road slowed us down. Finally we arrived in Bamenda late afternoon. From the mountain overlooking the city, we could see the valley and the numerous columns of smoke rising from fires used to cook in the backyard of the homes. The entire valley was covered with a cloud of smoke which looked like smog all over the city. Never would I have expected to see such pollution in Africa, a continent where nature is omnipresent with countries that are hardly industrialized. The scene greatly surprised everyone in our group of travellers. Once we reached the valley in the centre of the city, this phenomenon was less visible, but the smell of smoke was everywhere. Around 5 pm we finally arrived at the hotel, a beautiful five-story building built in the shape of stairs. Decidedly, the architect had worked hard to give it a modern look.

In the great entrance hall, Barry, who had been distributing the keys, informed us that there was not enough electricity to operate the elevators. So, we would have to carry our luggage up the stairs ourselves. He told us to meet back there in 30 minutes. There was a celebration for the region's king at his residence; we were late and they were waiting for us. While waiting for my suitcase, I ordered a beer at the hotel bar. After endless hours on the bus without air conditioning, this beer was highly appreciated. When our luggage finally arrived, Marie-Andrée Laflamme suggested to her husband, Jean-Hugues, that she will take care of our beer while we took the bags to our rooms. In semi-darkness up we went the stairs leading to our rooms. We ran out of breath quickly and as soon as we had finished we started laughing at the situation.

Upstairs there was no light in the hallways; there was only the light from a window at the end of the hallway that provided some visibility. It was so dim that we could hardly distinguish the numbers on the doors. I finally got to my room and I looked for the handle so I could put the key in. Guess what - no handle. I found the lock and inserted the key, then I turned it and the door opened. Since the curtains had been drawn it was very dark in the room and I had to go looking for the light switch. I was finally able to turn on a feeble lamp near the bed, located at the back of the room, which only emitted a little light. I put my suitcase down and immediately went to the window to draw the curtains open. But the opening mechanism was broken and they refused to move. I found the balcony door behind them, but the sweltering heat from outside quickly made me change my mind. I finished inspecting my palace by having a look at the bathroom. A light bulb was hanging from the ceiling and it revealed a bathroom stripped of all its accessories. The toilet seat was on the floor leaning against the wall. There was a shower and a small thin towel that would clearly not suffice to properly dry my whole body.

After my summary inspection I sat on the bed for a bit because all I wanted to do was to relax a few minutes before joining the group. As soon as my butt touched the bed, I sank into the mattress that was incredibly soft and I fell backwards. My body was now shaped as a half moon, my buttocks several inches lower than my head and my feet. For twenty dollars a night, I probably should not have expected more.

After a long day's drive with terrible seats, and having been squeezed tightly with my colleagues in the uncomfortable minibus, with heat and humidity, suddenly this discomfort was starting to affect me. At this moment, I felt very far away from my country and my people. I also realised that in a few weeks, I would have to leave for a small remote village in Ecuador to study the feasibility of a water project. I found myself hoping that this other trip would turn out to have better conditions. All of a sudden, I could not wait to go back home.

Once again here we were in a minibus on our way to visit the king of the region. We turned onto a red dirt road, which was so characteristic of this part of Africa. After roughly ten minutes, the bus went up a small narrow street, and then stopped at the front door of an enclosure surrounded by a high fence. The one known as the queen had been waiting for us and she was angry because we were more than an hour late. They took us to a courtyard where the show was to take place. At the sound of the drums, a group of dancers invaded the centre of the square and started their show. Even though our hosts wanted to please us, I felt that this day trip was too much and I couldn't wait for it to end. The show finally ended and I slipped away to visit the grounds with the royal buildings. In the centre, perched on a promontory, the King's huge "castle" took up all the space. The two-story building seemed lost in this place that looked like a kingdom made of pasteboard. Finally someone signaled us that it was time to leave. Before reaching the exit, we had to pass in front of the inevitable vendors' souvenir tables. Fortunately, we were urged us to get back into our minibus as the local Rotary Club was expecting us for dinner.

We went back to the hotel where we attended a meeting organised by the Bamenda Rotary Club. According to tradition, we exchanged banners from our respective clubs, and then we enjoyed a friendly dinner with some members of the club who were happy to greet foreign visitors. The dinner ended around nine o'clock and we were all pleased to return to our rooms, as the next day we would have to repeat the journey in reverse in order to catch our flight late at night in Douala. The next morning at seven o'clock, everyone met in the dining room. Soon, word got around that the process of paying for the room was quite lengthy.

As soon as I finished eating breakfast, I headed to the reception desk to pay my bill. The young clerk was trying to understand an English-speaking colleague in front of me. After translating for them, it was my turn, so I gave my name and room number. The clerk took out a pack of bills and with slow meticulous gestures he inserted three pages of carbon paper between the bills to make copies. Everything was done manually and he even wrote my name in beautiful calligraphy, but this was also done with incredible slowness. My blood pressure was rising, but I was able to control myself. Then he recorded my passport number at an equally slow pace as well as my room number and the cost of the room. And to confirm that nothing would be added to the bill, he took out a ruler and drew a line sideways on the page, which would record the total of my bill: twenty dollars. Then, not to tear the bill, he slowly and carefully detached the page from the tablet. Phew, he finally finished, I said to myself. But imagine my surprise when I saw him pull out an accounting tablet on which he started writing the same information all over again!

- Why are you starting over? I asked.

- Sir, it's for accounting, he said, as he continued to write the information down.

My impatience was growing as fast as the line of my colleagues behind me. Next, he handed me a receipt that I refused because I had no need for it. All in all, I had been here for nearly ten minutes. If it were to take that long for each of my thirty colleagues behind me, we would still been there at noon. As I was one of the few francophones in our group, I decided to intervene. I explained to the young man that we did not need bills and that we had to leave, because we had a long way to go ahead of us. The poor man continued to insist because his boss required that records be well kept. I then explained the situation to my friends and I collected money by taking note of their room number. I handed the list and the amount of money to the young man who was shocked at the situation. After adding everything up, I took a blank sheet of paper on which I wrote a receipt for the total to be paid and I asked the young cashier to sign it.

We finally hit the road, because while we were waiting to pay, the drivers had had plenty of time to load our luggage on the roof. The group was now happier than the day before, because we knew that our destination was the Douala airport and that our trip was really coming to an end. Now at the airport, while we were waiting in groups for Air France's counter to open, police prowled around us and kept looking at us curiously. Suddenly, one of them came up to me and asked me what I had inside my bag. I showed him a frame that I had bought at the market. He then asked me to follow him. I asked why; he just said he worked for Customs and I had to pay a fee to get my frame out of the country. I'm not sure that these officers really did work for Cameroon Customs. Being skeptical, I explained to my colleagues in English what was happening and without much enthusiasm I decided to follow the two policemen.

They led me to an office on the second floor and I asked them why I was the only one paying the tax. Next, I explained that in all the countries of the world, customs fees were normally collected at the entrance of the country and not when people left. I thought it was unfair to have to pay customs because by purchasing this frame at the market, I had contributed to the local economy and in addition I had been there as a volunteer to vaccinate against polio. Nothing I said could change their minds. I had to pay customs for my frame. Finally, once I was out of arguments, I decided to pay the equivalent of thirty-five dollars that they had ask me for in CFA francs. I went back to join the group and I then informed them of my misadventure. I advised them to hide their luggage so they would not have to pay customs. Thus I left Cameroon with the feeling that I had been conned by these two police officers.

5

THIS TIME, I SAW AFRICA!

Cat In A Hurry...

Two years later, I joined the group headed by Barry Howie and his wife, Jane, once again for the national polio immunization campaign. This time we were off to Burkina Faso and Togo. Ever since the trip to Cameroon, I had been left unsatisfied as I felt that I had not really seen Africa. We spent most of our time in the immediate area surrounding Douala, a large industrial city, with the exception of our trip to Bamenda which mainly consisted of a bus ride lasting several hours. Visiting only one region of this vast continent was not enough. I wanted to see more.

When we arrived in Ouagadougou, the capital of Burkina Faso, we were greeted again by Bawa Mankoube, Vice President of the African campaign against polio. Bawa met us in the international arrivals section. He organised our passage through immigration where they stamped our passports without asking any questions. He asked a group of porters to load our suitcases. As soon as a Customs officer wanted to further check on our luggage, Bawa intervened, telling him that we were there to vaccinate against polio. It was one of the easiest passages through customs ever since September 2001.

The trip had been planned for a long time and our airline tickets had been booked well in advance. One week before our departure, Burkina Faso decided, for reasons that I was not aware of, to delay the immunization days. Taken aback, organisers turned to Togo which holds its NIDs roughly the same dates as those to be held in Burkina Faso. To occupy us the day before the start of the vaccination in Togo, and to please us, our friend Bawa suggested a detour through the Arly National Reserve located in southwestern Burkina Faso, on the border of Togo and Benin. This detour, a distance of a few dozen kilometres, allowed us to see a natural reserve and even take safari photos.

The day after our arrival was a day off because the organisers had declared a day of rest for us due to jet lag. As we arrived at the hotel late at night, the rest was quite appreciated. We took this opportunity to visit the area around our hotel in the centre of Ouagadougou. Some went to the bank to change dollars into CFA francs. I decided to have a look at the market located nearby. I could see no one outside, but as soon as I stepped outside of the hotel, a horde of young peddlers flocked towards me trying to sell me their worthless objects. These poor children were desperate for customers, but what they had to offer did not interest me. Even though I told them that I was not interested, they continued to follow me when I crossed the street. Fortunately, the farther I got from the hotel, the more their numbers diminished. By the time I got to the market, only one young boy about ten years old had managed to continue following me. So, I asked him questions about what I was observing and he provided answers. Then, he guided me through the maze of alleys so I did not get lost. After a moment, I said:

- It's nice to guide me and tell me things, but you will not make a lot of money by following me here in the market.

- Sir, he replied with a grin, here in Burkina Faso we have a saying: «The cat in a hurry never catches the mouse»!

In short, he had just given me a great sales lesson. With patience, we get what we want. And what do you think happened when we got back to the hotel? Well Yes, I bought a piece of cloth from him that had a scene of African life on it, which he had proposed to me right from the moment I had left the hotel. The cat had caught the mouse!

I felt like I had let him take advantage of me, not because I had spent money on something that had little or of no interest for me, but mostly because a young African had just lectured me in a way. The three dollars that the piece of cloth cost me was insignificant, but it represented so much for this young boy. Given the time he spent serving as my guide, I considered that he had earned the three dollars. I did not even negotiate, as is the custom. Today, this piece hangs on the wall of my office and I still remember this young determined salesman.

A Mother Teresa from Germany

Some members of the group had organised a visit to an orphanage for the middle of the afternoon in which Canadians had collaborated and I decided to join them. Several of us had brought suitcases of clothes, medicines, toiletries, books and various little things that make our lives easier, but that were often missing in Africa.

Our driver had a hard time finding the place. In this poor neighbourhood of Ouagadougou, street names were not posted, and our bus had to constantly go around piles of dirt, potholes or piles of trash that had been left in the middle of the street. After searching for several minutes, we finally arrived at the AMPO orphanage. The director was waiting for us on the street corner. Seeing the bus arrived, she opened up the doors of the enclosure so the driver could get in.

We were greeted by its founding director, a German woman named Katrin Rhodes. She was a successful business woman in her country; she decided to sell her bookstore chain in order to devote her life to the children living in the streets of Ouagadougou. It all began modestly twenty years ago and she was now responsible for more than three hundred children.

As soon as we got off the bus, they took us to a shaded area under a shelter which had large wooden tables. We all sat down to listen to Katrin explain the operation of the AMPO orphanage. While she spoke, the kids came instinctively to her and Katrin responded by cuddling them and caressing their hair with her hands. Just looking at her you quickly realised that these children were hers. She was not just the director of an orphanage which was her livelihood. No, she was the mother of this large family and such unconditional love really impressed me.

As we had lost a lot of time looking for the orphanage, we agreed to come back when we would get back to Ouagadougou for our flight. Then we would be able see in greater detail the various workshops of the orphanage where young people were learning a trade. Those who had brought equipment gave their suitcases to Katrin and we said goodbye. We left after promising to return.

But Where Is Arly?

The next morning we set off for Togo, our final destination. As the change of dates had given us some free time, we decided to drive to the Arly National Reserve. Our group split into two minibuses and our luggage was secured on the roof; I can say that the suspension took quite a beating. Although we were a bit cramped and despite the heat, we remained in a good mood. The air conditioning was not enough to keep the interior cool and every time the driver started the AC, the engine tended to overheat, so we decided to open the windows to create air circulation instead.

Around noon, we stopped to eat in a small town. The driver knew a little restaurant right off the main road. The place did not look like much, but it seemed to be the best in the area. Not being very inspired by the location and true to my policy on food when I travel, I was content with a piece of baguette and a cold beer. I decided to eat my baguette with the group that took refuge in the garden under the shade of mango trees. Some had ventured to eat chicken and I wished them well hoping they wouldn't get sick. There is nothing more effective than gastroenteritis to take away your desire to travel.

We were enjoying the air in the shade under the mango trees, but we had to go back to our seats in the minivans. As soon as the driver put the vehicle in reverse, we heard a loud noise followed by the crash of broken glass. We had just backed up into a metal post and the rear window of the van had been shattered. Fortunately, no one was hurt; there was more concern than harm. All we had to do was to repair the damage.

Obviously, in this small town, there were no vendors of minibus parts! We had to find an alternative so we could continue our journey. In the corner of a garage, the driver found a roll of plastic which he quickly turned into a rear window. After more than half an hour of waiting, we got back on the bus, but this time it made an additional noise: the plastic clapping in the wind.

The ride was supposed to take about four hours, but we were told that in Africa often double the time was needed. So, when the end of the afternoon came, we were not too surprised to still be far from our destination. However, the situation only deteriorated once we had turned onto a dirt road. Our minibus raised a cloud of red dust that seeped through the doors and the broken window, which made breathing difficult. Those who were sitting in the front were not too bothered, but the more you were sitting toward the back, the more the air was difficult to breath.

That's when a passenger, a nurse by profession, remembered that she had a certain amount of masks in her luggage. We were now sitting in this cramped and overheated space, masked as surgeons performing a delicate operation. Even though it was uncomfortable, the masks made our breathing easier. Since we were tired, the sight of our fellow masked friends just made us laugh and jokes began to roll. Our good spirits had returned right up until our driver stopped the vehicle in the middle of nowhere in the bush. A rear tire had deflated: it had to be changed.

This unexpected stop allowed us to stretch our legs and breathe fresh air free of dust. Thus, we got out one by one and it was confirmed that the more you were sitting toward the back, the more you were covered with red dust. The masks, which initially had been pristine white, had turned red. Our clothes had also turned completely red, so much so that when I emptied my bags, I had to soak and wash my pants twice to get them back to their original colour.

But this was not the end of our misery. The driver had managed with difficulty to replace the defective tire. In the meantime, the other minibus went by without even noticing our driver flashing his lights. When the tire repair was finished, we continued and it was with some concern that we realised that our driver was not sure which route to take to get to the Arly reserve. A little farther, we happily joined our friends in the other van that had stopped to wait for us. But their driver did not know where the famous reserve was either...

We had been in darkness for a long time by now. At each intersection, the driver hesitated and finally our host Bawa had to make the decisions. Then we started to worry that we would run out of fuel. Thankfully, we saw a gas station at an intersection, which provided our drivers with the opportunity to ask for directions. We finally arrived at the entrance of the reserve at 11:30 pm, and we were tired and hungry as it had now been more than ten hours since we left the small restaurant.

The camp consisted of small clay huts, some with air conditioning. Since I was the last person to get my key, I did not have an air-conditioned room but I didn't care, all I needed was a good bed. It wasn't too long before everyone ended up at the bar to enjoy our usual drink, a cold beer. What a delight! Some took the opportunity to jump into the pool, even though the water was not very clear. I abstained and when they announced that the pizza was ready, we had all been literally starving so it was with great pleasure that we sat down to eat.

After finishing the meal, I headed to my hut which was absolutely stifling. This was normal, because the mercury had climbed up to 47 during the day. I lay on my bed, but I was having trouble getting to sleep and my pillow quickly got soaked with sweat. My roommate, Michael Cheng, from Toronto of Chinese descent, managed to fall asleep before me. I was still trying to fall asleep when all of a sudden I heard that our guide, Bawa, was looking for a place to spend the night. Since there was space in our hut, I invited him to share it with us. An employee brought him a mattress which we then installed on the floor in a corner. So, here I was, a Quebecker spending my first night in a hut in the heart of Africa with a Chinese partner and our host who was originally from Togo. Despite the difficult conditions of the journey, I appreciated the situation as it proved to me that, whatever our origins, we all needed the same thing: a good night's sleep.

It was a tough night though. Barely half an hour after Bawa had settled down, the camp turned off the electricity, which in effect stopped the fan. It was one heck of a hot night; there was not even the slightest breeze to cool our house down whose door was left wide open despite the possible presence of small animals. Since I was unable to sleep, I got up and went out to get some fresh air. It was hot, but much less so than inside the hut. When fatigue overcame me again, I went back to my bed and fell soundly asleep until five in the morning, at which time we had to get up if we wanted to participate in a photo safari organised specially for us.

One by one, the participants in the safari exited their hut, eyes still full of sleep. After breakfast, we met in the parking lot where the all-terrain vehicles were waiting. The sun was still low and the temperature quite pleasant. Our caravan headed out and guides led us to the African Savannah. Since it was the dry season, we saw few animals. From time to time, we caught a glimpse of an antelope or other small animals. Our guide stopped the jeep to show us an elephant trail. Even though we didn't actually see any, their tracks were impressive. The series of large footprints left by their massive paws fired my imagination.

Further along, our guides led us near a river where a rhino family romped. While the whole group was observing the animals in the river, I noticed that one of our guides turned his back to us and scanned the area, gun in hand, ready to fire. I then realised that the African Savannah can be dangerous. I asked him the reason for this concern. "What is so dangerous?"

He explained that a few weeks ago, during the visit of a French minister, he had to use his gun to ward off a threatening lion. He did not want to take any chances. After his comments, I was very happy to return to the jeep. We continued our trek through the savannah till 9 am. The sun was high and it was already hot.

Once everybody had picked up their belongings, we were off to Togo. We arrived at the border in mid-afternoon. A long line of trucks stretched on either side of the road; they needed their papers to enter Togo. As I was the only francophone in the group, I was nominated to meet the customs agents in Burkina Faso with everyone's passport to officially register our departure from the country. The officer in charge took each passport and registered in a great book the holder's name, date of birth, nationality and passport number. As everything is done by hand, it took nearly an hour to complete the formalities. Meanwhile, my friends who got off the bus to stretch their legs made the acquaintance of a young girl crawling on the ground. She was a polio victim and her legs were severely affected.

Two physiotherapists in the group were intrigued to see the deformed limbs of this young woman. They wondered if it was still possible to do something for her. They asked her a few questions and took photographs of her atrophied limbs, promising to try to improve her condition. Upon their return home, they contacted several hospitals and organisations including Shriners only to be told that, unfortunately, given the degree of deformity and the age of the young woman, it was already too late to perform reconstructive surgery. I hope that this young woman has not added us to the ordeal she already endures. I learned from this experience that we must be very careful not to create high expectations among the people we want to help. If we manage to do something for them, that's great, but if not, we must not add to their misfortune by promising them things that we are not certain to be able to deliver.

Once the departure formalities were completed in Burkina Faso, we got back on the bus to cross the hundred yards separating us from Togo. Here, a simple wooden hut equipped with a counter served as the border crossing. Over time, the accumulation of dirt on the road resulted in the customs officers being about one metre lower than the passengers across the counter. Again, they needed to record manually all the information in the passports. During our stop at the border of Burkina Faso, our guide Bawa contacted our Togolese friends. One of them arrived and offered to take our passports and bring them to back to us in Dapaong. Since we were expected at our destination and already behind schedule, it was agreed that this was the best way to proceed. Some members of the group were worried about leaving their passport with a stranger, but eventually we all agreed and continued our journey.

Our stay in Togo was very different from what we had experienced in Cameroon two years before. Instead of bringing us to the villages to vaccinate from door to door, we did what is called social mobilization. This meant that they were going to use us to promote the beginning of the vaccination campaign. Thus, the next day we participated in the launch of the campaign along with the Togo health authorities. After the usual speeches, some were administered vaccines before we left the area to go to another village where once again we participated in the launch of the vaccination operation. The entire week proceeded in this manner.

We were led to Dapaong, Sansané-Mango, Kara and Sokode before heading to Sinkasé, a border town with Burkina Faso. In all these cities, we were warmly welcomed by the local population. As we moved from one village to another, our contacts with the public were quite limited. However, we were able to talk to members of the Rotary Clubs of Kara and Dapaong. As for our group leader, Barry, and yours truly who are former governors of our Rotary district, we were required to travel in the personal car of our host, Bawa, who had brought along his driver from the capital, Lome, more than six hundred kilometres away. Our sitting arrangements were even worse than they had been in the minibus, jammed as we were in the back of the car. Fortunately, our absence on the bus freed up valuable space for our companions who were not eligible for the same honour as us—an honour that I would have gladly done without. But as Africans are people with protocol, hierarchy must be respected!

Back in AMPO

A week later, we were back in Ouagadougou. Since our flight was not until the evening, part of our group took advantage of the waiting time to return to AMPO to see Katrin and visit the classrooms. She received us in the girls' house, across the street from where she had received us a week earlier. After serving us a soft drink, she took out a flashlight and some insect repellent spray in small format from her bag and said: "I have a favour to ask. Let

99

me know if you have any objections that I keep this flashlight for myself. It would be very helpful for me to see the children at night when we run out of electricity. Also, the format of this mosquito repellent would allow me to put it in my bag when I go to visit our farm in the countryside. I know you brought these things for the kids, but it would be very useful. "

We accepted, of course. Her honesty and generosity impressed me greatly. I do not know many people who would have asked permission to take these objects. For me, this application was further evidence of the altruism of this exceptional woman. Listening to Katrin talk about her children and seeing her act, she reminded me of Mother Teresa.

After visiting a carpentry shop, a welding shop, a sewing shop and others, we said goodbye to Katrin after giving her the rest of the money in CFA francs that we could not bring with us because it was not possible to exchange them outside the country. Others took the opportunity to donate to the orphanage. But that day, the best gift for us was meeting this very special woman. We left, wondering what more we could do to help. James Bradley followed up this visit with the help of some other Rotary Club members from Ottawa and sent a new welding machine for the welding shop. This would allow the young people to learn with new equipment and would make it possible for them to enter the labour market having already worked with the latest equipment. Other members of the group were also instrumental in helping the orphanage.

This would not be the only gesture of James Bradley and his wife, Linda. Two years later, Linda provided Katrin with a great opportunity to raise money for AMPO.

I Return to Ouagadougou

Linda Bradley, who was present during the first trip to Ouagadougou, brought Katrin Rhodes to Canada in 2006 as a keynote speaker for a meeting of members of her Rotary District where I was also a speaker. On this occasion, Katrin was able to meet several donors and raise money for AMPO. As this meeting occurred just weeks before I left for my second trip to Burkina Faso, I took the opportunity to ask Katrin what her children needed most. I passed this information on to my future travel companions and, six weeks later, I arrived at the orphanage with a group of twenty-five Quebeckers, bringing with them thirty bags of materials for Katrin's kids.

Katrin told me that her kids were in great need of baseball caps for protection against the sun while working in the fields. So I called my friends from different Rotary Clubs in the region of Quebec City and in less than a week, I had collected over three hundred hats, most of which were new baseball caps with different logos from companies or sports teams or from clothing manufacturers. They came in a wide range of colours!

That day, it was party time at the orphanage. Each member of the group gave Katrin the equipment they brought. Each time we opened a suitcase, it was a pleasure to see how delighted Katrin and her kids were. In addition to baseball caps, the suitcases contained books, balls, soccer jerseys, flashlights, clothing, etc. Everyone had their picture taken with Katrin and the children to keep a memory of that magical moment. It is often said that it is better to give than to receive. I can assure you that on that day, the donors were happy.

The children sang songs to thank us and it is with wide smiles that they banged on their drums, each song ending with a round of applause and laughter. As it had been the case on the first trip, group members asked to return to visit the orphanage before flying back home.

Togo, I'm Back!

Among the group of twenty-five Quebeckers who accompanied me on this journey, I was the only one who had set foot in Africa before. For them, it was like discovering another world. Certainly, they had all seen images of Africa on TV, but being there, feeling the heat and seeing up close the conditions in which Africans live was a different story.

As before, we left Ouagadougou by bus, but this time we travelled in a large bus that was lent to us by a private school in Dapaong. The trip ran smoothly especially since I avoided visiting the Arly reserve.

At Dapaong, I booked the entire Caroli hotel for the group, for $30 per room. We settled in for the week. Arsene Tindame, a Rotarian friend who was in charge of organising the trip there had prepared a full agenda. The first day was spent visiting various authorities one after the other before going to the Yendube Children's Hospital for the official presentation of a blood analyzer for AIDS victims. This unit was purchased through the pooling of funds raised by all participants of the previous trip. The device which cost more than $35,000 was paid for by Rotary Clubs in Canada, the United States and Australia. With the help of a grant from the Rotary Foundation of Rotary International, the necessary amount had been raised and the unit was able to be purchased. Sister Genevieve, the director of the hospital, waited for my second visit to formalize the delivery of the unit. This was a truly international project from donors of three countries on two continents who had come together to realise a project in a fourth country on a third continent. A fascinating accomplishment!

After the official ceremonies and all the protocol typical of Africa, we were invited to visit the hospital. For us it was a real shock. The hospital was full of people: patients and visitors. The large porch of the main building served as a waiting room. There were no private or semi-private rooms, only large rooms with small metal beds lining the walls where patients, visitors and caregivers mingled together. All these rooms had large openings onto corridors for air circulation and to prevent the heat from becoming unbearable inside. From the corridors, we had a direct view of the sick children and their parents on hand to support them. There was no privacy. Such a situation would be inadmissible in North America, but here it seemed to be the norm.

Several members of the group were unable to complete the visit because they found it unbearable. Some took pictures, a gesture that offended others who called it voyeurism. Some even asked me to intervene and stop them from taking pictures. Others hid away to not show their emotions. I saw tears streaming down the faces of some. Taking pictures is always a sensitive issue. It should always be done with discretion and discernment. These photos were not to be used as hunting trophies, but as ways to educate those around us about the misery of others.

Before leaving the hospital, a member of the group was photographed with a child to whom he gave a teddy bear offered by his own children. Another member, a surgeon by profession, asked to visit the operating room and later stated that he believed that operating in those conditions was comparable to operating in his own garage at home. Africa can be very shocking. For all of us, the hospital visit was a painful experience on the first day.

Even though this was my second visit to the Yendube hospital, I still felt the same discomfort. The sight of all this misery made you feel utterly useless. At least this time, by giving them the blood analyzer on behalf of the group of 2005, I was able to help a little.

Sister Genevieve gave us a list of equipment that the hospital needed to improve its laboratory. The group was consulted and people spontaneously put their hands in their pocket and quickly collected a sum of about $3,000, enough for Sister Genevieve to purchase one of the units on her list.

We Will Vaccinate in Savannah

After visiting the hospital, we went to a village to proceed with the inauguration of a well, a project funded by a Rotary Club in Canada. To thank us for our visit, the villagers gave us a goat, a gift of great significance for the people who live in poor conditions. We tried to explain that we could not bring a goat back to Canada, but in vain. To refuse the goat would have been an insult, so we left for our hotel with an additional passenger in the bus. The poor frightened animal left visible traces of his presence. We ended up giving the goat to Sister Genevieve at the Yendube hospital we had visited earlier. We were told that the goat would be at the heart of the feast prepared for children at Christmas.

The following days were spent on vaccination which was the real purpose of our visit. Arsene Tindame, the former president of the Dapaong Rotary Club who organised the visit, brought us to his home village. This remote village on a rocky plateau of the Savannah region was over a hundred feet above the plain.

As our bus was too big to climb up to the plateau, we piled into two vans. Some of our African companions sat on the roof to make the journey with us. As soon as we began the climb, the road that led to the village of Nagou became narrower to the point of becoming a trail hidden by tall grass. Arriving at the end of the trail, our drivers asked us to get off the vans and walk the rest of the way. Thus a long queue of thirty people was formed, swirling around in the savannah between the tall grass, and moving toward the small village.

The weather was humid, hot and this simple march was quite a test for some of my companions. However, enthusiasm reigned as women from the village welcomed us with a dance. The village chief then brought us to a field at the entrance of the village in order to sacrifice a chicken as an incantation to the good spirits. He cut the chicken's neck and poured milk over the blood as it spilled on the ground. He then dropped the chicken that ran awkwardly around as it was not yet dead. The higher it jumped, the more auspicious it was thought to be. That morning, it moved energetically which seemed to appeal to our hosts who applauded with delight. The vaccination could now begin!

Each team member was paired with a Togolese who knew the area. Each team was assigned a territory and off we went on the trails in search of children to vaccinate. We went from one hut to another by walking on trails bordered by very tall grass, taller than us. From time to time, at the intersection of a trail, we met another team going in the opposite direction. We took the time to exchange information on homes that had been visited and off we went again. In less than two hours, we covered the entire village and we returned to the centre of the village where the women prepared a meal for us.

We were served guinea fowl which had been cooked at length on a wood fire. We sought some shade because the heat was overwhelming. After walking in the sun, some faces had turned a bright red. Others even found a way to get a little sleep in the shade of a large baobab tree.

After the meal, the women treated us to more dancing, then it was our turn to give them a gift. We had brought a suitcase full of medication that we gave to the person responsible for the health of the village.

Pleased with this unexpected gift, the person asked if there were drugs in the suitcase that could treat two children who were sick. Dr. Céline Benoit, a doctor who accompanied us, asked to see the children immediately. One of them had a terrible toothache and she gave the health official a prescription that would help. The other child had a high fever. Again, medication was provided.

These two children were lucky that we happened to be in their village that day. I wonder what happened under normal circumstances. How do you relieve a toothache when there are no drugs? How do you relieve a child's fever? All of us have medication in our homes to relieve these problems. But how do these people manage without drugs? Without a vehicle in this high-altitude village, access to a doctor must not be easy. And to think that we complain about our health care system because we have to wait a little!

Before returning to our bus, our friend Arsene brought us to the trail that women used to fetch water in the savannah. As the village was perched high, it was not easy to go down that path. They had to descend by jumping from one rock to the other, while avoiding slipping, and sometimes it was even necessary to use a tree trunk as a ladder to negotiate a steeper section. I tried to make my way for a few yards, trying not to slip and fall between the rocks, but when I came to the tree trunk, I gave up! It was simply too dangerous for me. How in the world, I wondered, did these women manage to climb up with a jug of water on their head? They had to be in exceptionally good shape to accomplish this feat day after day. Fortunately, I learned two years later that the villagers had managed to dig a well and find water on this high plateau.

Arsene continued to serve as our guide and bought us to a very special place which explained the presence of the village on the plateau. On the cliff overlooking the plain, there was a ledge a few metres wide and, in certain places, deep under the rocks, large caves had formed that served as exceptional shelters. Villagers used this ledge to shelter their families when enemy tribes tried to invade their village. Everyone went down to the ledge and could thus hide from their pursuers. By removing the ladders, the enemies were unable to reach them. Today it could be easily accessed via a metal staircase. All along the ledge, you could see large jugs of sandstone that were used to hold water. Traces of fire for cooking were still visible. From here, the view of the valley was absolutely beautiful, but the people came here to survive not for the view!

We returned to the hotel and that night all the members of the team, although worn out by the heat, were very satisfied with their day, the difficult road they had travelled and the emotions they had experienced. Some even mentioned that if the trip were to end then and there, they would be completely satisfied.

For my part, I was also tired, because as a group leader, I was the last one to bed and it was up to me to sound the alarm at six o'clock in the morning. Added to this was the fact that my friend Arsene had the habit of knocking on my door in the middle of the night because he had forgotten something or because he needed money to pay for this or that. Luckily, André Pomerleau, a caterer by profession, was among us and he had showed the hotel cooks how to prepare a good breakfast. Quite a change from the cold omelets we were served on our first morning there. This was indeed a beneficial professional exchange. Hopefully the cook would use this new knowledge for future hotel guests.

A Blind Orphan in Savannah

The next day, we changed villages again to continue our vaccination work. This time, we went to the village of Nano. As it was larger, we needed more time to cover the whole territory, but we managed even to include the crowded market. Late in the morning, the teams arrived one after the other in the centre of the village where a giant baobab provided shade for the whole group. The sweltering heat was over 40 degrees.

After inaugurating a new well, they took us to a place near the school where they laid the first stone of a future college. Then they gave me a boubou, the garment that all Africans wear and, surprisingly, it turned out to be heavy and hot. At the same time, I was appointed honorary chief of the village.

Africans really love their protocol, as I have already mentioned. In each village we always had to contend with various ceremonies. That day, after the meal and once the mandatory protocol had been duly completed, the group joined the students in the courtyard. A teacher was accompanied by a student roughly twelve years old. He told us that on top of being half blind, the young boy was orphaned and he currently had no place to stay and no one to care for him.

As he told us his story, we were quickly surrounded by several adults and children of the village. The teacher asked us if we could do something for him because, despite his disability, he was interested in pursuing his studies.

One group member, Clément Gaudreau from Montmagny, decided to use some of the money he had received from his club before leaving to help the boy. We agreed that three people, including the teacher, would be appointed as guardians of the money and that it would be used exclusively to pay for young boy's room and board as well as his tuition.

These were very moving moments for Clément and me. It seemed so easy to help in a country with so many poor people. A few hundred dollars sufficed to give hope and a brighter future to the young orphan.

For me and I am convinced that this was also true for Clément, this was one of the magical moments of this trip. I saw Clément recently and he still remembers the smile on the young Togolese boy's face as he learned that he would be able to pursue his dream of going to school. That day, he had made a difference in the life of this young student—and it had also changed his life forever. Moments like these are rare. Often we help, but are not able to see up close and personal the impact of our actions.

We finished our mission and it was time to hit the road back to Ouagadougou. A member of the group, very affected by the heat to the point of not being able to leave his room all week, found the trip back to be particularly difficult. His companions helped him throughout the long hours of travel to Ouagadougou. I think that for him, Africa was over!

On our way back, we decided to stop at the Sofitel in Ouagadougou. I felt that my companions needed to enjoy a little comfort before returning home. Our driver asked how much it cost for a room at the five-star hotel. He was shocked to learn that the price was $160 per night, which was more than he earned in a month! Needless to say, it made us realise once again how lucky we were...

Once installed at the hotel, I noticed how easy it was to reconnect with comfort. Some enjoyed a swim in the pool, others visited the bar or the local market. After a nap, I met with some members of the group at the pool. The cool beer was very refreshing. I was soon overcome with fatigue as the stress of being crew chief started dissipating. However, the journey was not over yet, there remained much to do. The next day, before flying home, we would return as promised to the AMPO orphanage.

This visit proved to be very emotional. Katrin greeted us in the shade on the balcony of the small administrative building of the orphanage. Before leaving home, members of the group asked their friends and their Rotary Club to help these people by giving their gifts to Katrin one after the other. These were moments of pure emotion for the donor and Katrin. Even the accountant for the orphanage was touched. After each gift, he brought the money to his office. Afterward, he was smiling ear to ear as he informed us that we had given in excess of $4,500!

This tidy sum, added to the money she had collected during her trip to Canada, would allow Katrin to complete the irrigation well on the land used by the farm school at the orphanage. Due to a lack of time, we were not able to visit this farm school located an hour's drive from Ouagadougou, but Katrin sent me pictures of the well a few months later, which I shared with the group members. These photos were of the metal structure that workers were erecting as well as the completed work. In all the pictures we could see the kids proudly wearing the hats that we gave them.

I had the chance to meet Katrin Rhodes on five occasions and each time I was impressed by her generosity with "her" children. For me it was a perfect example of giving of oneself. She could have continued to live comfortably in Europe, retained her stores and simply supported an organisation of her choice which worked with orphans and street children. Instead she preferred to leave everything and move to the heart of the action in Ouagadougou and invest fully in her life's work: the AMPO orphanage. She lives modestly in difficult conditions, suffering from malaria... But she surely would have missed the love from all these children!

The next day at the airport, I realised that the trip had taken its toll on my patience. I'm usually pretty tolerant when travelling, but I found myself reacting strongly to a rather widespread African attitude that really gets on my nerves: the bad habit of constantly begging for money.

Even in the highlands of Togo, I was shocked to realise that children in remote villages, who do not often see white people, instinctively stretched out their hand to beg. So, after a long wait at the airport in Ouagadougou, while sitting on the floor searching for pocket change to buy a soda, a young adult reached out and asked me for a few pieces of change. My reaction was instantaneous. I yelled at him aggressively: "What have you done to deserve any money from me?"

Pierre Barrette, a group member who works as a psychologist in Val-d'Or, immediately tried to calm me down. I quickly regretted my reaction that I attribute to fatigue. Thinking about it later, I can only assume that the imperialist attitude that Africans have been subjected to for centuries has left its mark. For many, white people are considered to be providers; just ask.

Finally, the departure bell rung and we left. Today, it is with certain nostalgia that I look back on this trip. I recently bumped into Pierre, the psychologist from Val-d'Or, whom I had not seen since 2007, and we recalled with pleasure some of the highlights of this trip. Here I must pay tribute to all those who made this journey with me. They were an absolutely wonderful group and I would leave again tomorrow morning without hesitation with each one of them for a new adventure in Africa!

6

MONGOLIA

Trees in the Sand!

After completing my term as Governor in 2003, I developed a taste for international projects. So I continued to take care of the Rotary Foundation in our district and to monitor projects that we supported in South America and Africa. Over the years, I therefore developed an expertise in this area, which allowed me to register as a member of the stewardship for the Rotary Foundation. The foundation was recruiting volunteers with professional experience in various sectors. The needs of these sectors included drinking water, education, health and financial audit. As a financial planner by profession, I registered in the category of financial auditing.

I had completed the registration forms for the program at least eighteen months earlier after receiving an email titled: Invitation to Serve. This is the peculiar way that the foundation invites us to accept a mission abroad. The foundation invites us, even though we are the ones who have volunteered. My first invitation was to inspect a tree planting project in Mongolia, specifically in the Gobi Desert.

As I opened this email, I could not believe my eyes. Generally, they invite Rotarians from neighbouring regions for these audits. I had to respond quickly and if I accepted I would have to leave no later than in three weeks, as I would have to produce the report of my visit in time for the trustees meeting of the Rotary Foundation taking place a few weeks from then... Mongolia is located between northern China and southern Siberia. It is a region of the world which is rarely visited and I would probably never have another opportunity to do so.

The invitation however, had come at a bad time. I was about to attend a one-week seminar in which I had enrolled several months ago. If I agreed to go to Mongolia, I would be away for another week and September was usually a busy month for my work. But the prospect of discovering the Gobi Desert was very exciting and I could not refuse. The few dollars in lost revenue during my absence would certainly not ruin me and after a few minutes of discussion with my wife, I accepted the invitation. I have never regretted that decision.

The following days were a real rat race as I now had to apply for my visa, make sure my travel dates were suitable for my hosts in Mongolia and for the international partners from South Korea. I also needed to contact the Rotary's travel agency to find seats at an acceptable price. Finally, it was Louise, my local travel agent, who ended up finding me tickets at a good price thus saving the Rotary Foundation several hundred dollars.

I received my invitation on September 5 and on the 16, I was on the plane to Ulaanbaatar, the capital of Mongolia. From Quebec, the trip takes well over 28 hours. Leaving on Sunday morning around 11 am, I arrived on Monday morning at 8:30 am after having stopped over in Montreal, Paris and Moscow. On top of this, we had to add on 13 hours of jet lag!

Upon exiting the plane and before stepping into the terminal I was greeted by Gandbold Erdene, a local Rotarian, who had been waiting for me. He was holding a sign with my name on it. After the usual introductions, he led me to a private VIP room where other members of the local Rotary Club were assembled. I was introduced to these people who had made a detour in order to greet me. Next, an airport attendant came to me and asked for my passport and my luggage tickets. We were served coffee and I got to know my colleagues from the local Rotary Clubs, the former governor Sang Koo Yun, the representative of the Korean Club, who financed the projects that I was to visit, Ganbat Erdene, Ganbold's brother. He would be our guide in the desert. There was also a young woman, Uyanga Tsakhilgaan, director of an English school in Ulaanbaatar who would accompany us throughout this journey. While we were still talking, the attendant came back to tell me that my luggage was near the exit of the lounge and she handed me back my passport.

As the formalities had already been dealt with, we left the room and went toward the exit. What a surprise to find out that our exit was directly on the tarmac right next to the aircraft that I had just arrived on. Then we all boarded the minibus which bypassed the terminal building and without further ado we were on our way to Ulaanbaatar.

At first glance, what surprised me most was the lack of vegetation. A few trees had been planted, but nothing else. The city had a typical architecture similar to that of the former Soviet Union. Everything was dull and gray. They dropped me off at my hotel, which was one of the best in the city, where I took a few hours off to relax. My hosts gave me a rendezvous a few hours later to attend a meeting concerning the projects with other members of the coordination committee who had not been able to come greet me at the airport.

Our first meeting took place around eleven o'clock. They described the projects to me over lunch at the restaurant. After our meal, we all boarded a van to go visit a village a few dozen kilometres from Ulaanbaatar. During this trip, I got a real taste of the local culture for the first time.

An Astonishing Tradition

The history of Mongolia is very rich, especially the period of Genghis Khan who conquered much of Asia in the twelfth century. His empire extended to northern China and also included Sogdiana, the region which includes Uzbekistan, Tajikistan and Afghanistan today. He is considered the father of the country by the Mongolian people. After his death, his empire was greatly expanded by his successors who ruled this territory for other hundred and fifty years.

Whenever Genghis Khan left for a military campaign with his many soldiers, each solider had the habit of throwing a stone at the foot of a wooden pole. Upon their return, each soldier would pick a stone up. The remaining stones thus gave an indication of the number of men killed in action. This explains the origin of ovoos, which eventually became a place of contemplation. Today we find many ovoos along the road. Blue ribbons are hung around the pole. It has also become a shamanic rite; it is customary to make three turns in a clockwise direction to ensure a good day. Locals leave offerings like seeds, money, milk and vodka. The ovoo is also a symbol of the link between earth and heaven.

After a short drive, once out of the city our bus stopped and everyone stepped out. It was at this point on the side of the road that they explained the ovoo tradition. I took advantage of the occasion to take photos of the area when all of a sudden, I saw our driver take out a bottle of vodka, open it and pour himself a drink. I got closer and then realised that this was part of the ritual. The driver poured a little vodka in a glass; he then poured a little on the ground to thank the Gods of the earth, then he threw a bit in the air to thank the Gods of heaven and, finally, he drank what was left. Since this was only a very small quantity, it did not affect his driving abilities. Although I was unaccustomed to drinking pure vodka, I willingly participated in the ritual. When everyone had finished drinking their few drops of vodka, together we all did our three ovoo turns before climbing back into the van and carrying on with our journey.

A few kilometres from a village that could be seen in the distance, the van started to slow down. The driver pulled over to the side of the road before coming to a complete stop in the desert. We stepped out and Sang Koo Yun and Gandbold explained to me that this is where they wanted to do their next project. We were on a plain; in fact we were already in the Gobi Desert. The project involved planting trees to build a natural barrier to the high winds that raise the desert dust and form dust clouds that can travel great distances. As a matter of fact, they pass over China, where they collect pollution and empty themselves in South Korea in the spring. This dust also travels to Japan and particles of it have even been found in the United States. The dust makes the air unbreathable. Moreover, since this trip, on at least two other occasions, I had the opportunity to read in my morning newspaper in Quebec, a paragraph mentioning the presence of these dust clouds that had invaded Seoul. It is for this reason that Koreans are so actively involved in this project.

While we were there, I could hear a train in the distance. On this vast plain, the horizon extended to infinity. Although the train was a few miles away, I could clearly see it looming on the horizon as if it were between heaven and earth. I had the impression of being in a portrait where the train represented the presence of man in this desert. I still remember this beautiful image.

We then continued our journey to the village to meet with the mayor and ask permission to carry out the project. He accepted and my friends even asked him to make gardens with the irrigation system that would be installed to water the newly planted trees. He was delighted by this, as there already was a community garden in the village, but a lack of water had resulted in poor crops.

Many nomads used to come to this village to trade and do some shopping, but what struck me the most were huge multi-story buildings that seemed to be abandoned just outside the city. They told me that these buildings were built by the Russians during the Soviet Union era and that during this period many Russians had lived in Mongolia. Although independent, the country aligned itself with the Soviet bloc which defended it against Japan during the 1939-1945 war.

We arrived in Ulaanbaatar and they brought me to visit a yurt, a round house used by nomads in the desert. This yurt was beautiful and well decorated, as it was a tourist attraction. I was told that I would have the opportunity to see more authentic ones in the desert. To wrap up the day, the whole group ended up in a Korean restaurant that our friend, Sang Koo wanted me to try out. Here, I discovered a simple yet exquisite cuisine. We would go back to this restaurant later in the week because the food was so delicious.

The City in the Middle of Nowhere

The next day we had to leave for Dalanzadgad, a town located about six hundred kilometres south of Ulaanbaatar and a few dozen kilometres from the northern border of China. This city is located in the Gobi Desert and Rotarians had already completed some plantation projects there. It was up to me to prepare a report on them as well as on some experiments that had been conducted in order to reduce the spread of the desert.

Again, when we arrived at the airport, we avoided the waiting room with ordinary travellers and were led instead to a VIP lounge. When we arrived in Dalanzadgad, the same scenario occurred again; we waited for our driver in the airport lounge. Even though the lounge was nothing fancy; the airport itself was very small and offered only minimal comfort. I discovered a small town of about fifteen thousand inhabitants who appeared to be bunched together for protection against the desert dust. House yards were surrounded by high fences that actually looked like barricades. We went around the city without stopping and then took the desert road westward to visit the projects.

They took us into what they called a "tourist camp", a collection of yurts used to house visitors. These were sort of a Mongolian version of a tourist cabin. A main building was used as a restaurant and for toilets. It was in this camp that I spent my first night in the desert.

In the Gobi Desert, it is ironic to talk about roads. They were rather like paths that had formed due to passing cars. Two tracks in the sand indicated that there was a road. Occasionally, the two tracks became four tracks parallel to each other so that vehicles could meet without having to slow down. Sometimes there was a change of direction. Each time, I wondered how the driver got his bearings, as there was no point of reference in the area. For me everything seemed the same; no trees, no mountains, nothing but small bushes trying to survive in the desert.

We finally arrived at the project site that I was to check out. This was a tree plantation which was seven kilometres long. It consisted of two sets of three rows of trees which were separated by a strip of land a few hundred metres wide. Each set of trees had been planted twenty metres apart and they reminded me of snow fences that we install in the fields along the roads in Quebec to stop blowing snow in the winter. The trees slow the wind down, which makes the dust settle and consequently prevents the winds from moving dust to moving to higher altitudes and travelling to other countries, including China, Korea and Japan.

Since native trees grew very quickly, they were the only ones planted. With adequate watering, the success rate of these plantations was excellent even though we were in the desert. Depending on the quality of work from those responsible for caring for the young plantations, the success rate varied from sixty to eighty-five percent. Obviously, wells had to be dug close to each plantation. In our first plantation, trees were already twice as tall as me, while on more recent plantation sites, the trees measured only a few dozen centimeters in height.

When I saw the vastness of the desert, I wondered about the true purpose of these plantations. This desert was so great that even though the rows of trees extended over seven kilometres, they still looked tiny. When arriving by plane, I had seen these long lines from the air, but they seemed so short. They explained to me that this project was part of the so-called "Mongolian Green Line" and, once they had been developed all over the country their impact would make a positive difference. You have to start somewhere, even though the work of men may look ridiculous in this vast desert.

During these travels, I discovered beautiful landscapes and I considered myself very lucky to be able to visit this region. At one point, our driver stopped on the edge of a cliff. From above, it was clear that the earth's crust had sunk tens of metres in the middle of this great plain. In moving closer to the edge of the cliff, I saw that the walls appeared to be solid red rock. The rock stood right out above the plains and, as the sun was about to set, the colours appeared even brighter. I walked along the cliff, for many minutes, so I could take in all this natural beauty. The sun was sinking fast and it was soon time to return to our camp for the night.

We took possession of our yurts and I shared mine with Sang Koo. Later, the whole group met at the main camp for dinner. This camp was a lot like a vacation camp with large wooden tables and a rustic decor. After a hearty meal, my friends decided to open a bottle of vodka. These descendants of nomads really knew how to have fun during long evenings in the desert. One after the other, they sang their native songs and good spirits prevailed. For a few songs, everyone got up and held up their mug. The group polished off at least two bottles before finally deciding to go to bed!

Our yurt was modestly furnished with two beds placed on each side of a small wood stove that sat in the middle of the room. At the head of our bed, there was a small piece of furniture painted red on which to set our belongings. When we returned to our yurt, the wood stove was already lit and the heat was comforting. We were at the end of September and the night was kind of cool. Besides, letting my hand slide down my bed I could feel the cold from outside that snuck in under the canvas.

Lying on my bed, I came to fully realise the situation that I was in: I was lying in a yurt, which is a typical dwelling of Mongolian nomads, in the middle of the Gobi Desert, accompanied by a Rotarian friend from South Korea. How lucky I was to belong to an organisation that allowed me to live through such experiences! I would never have imagined such a situation even in my wildest dreams. As I have already mentioned, when I was young I lived in a small village of forestry workers in New Brunswick, I wanted to travel the world, but that night I considered all my various travels and my incredible luck. I tried earnestly to fill my mind with memories, because when age would no longer allow me to travel the world, I would travel at leisure in my head. I will not regret taking the time and money to discover the world and its wonders.

The next day we visited other projects and I saw the site of a strange experiment that had gone wrong. The place was covered with dunes like those found in deserts. On some dunes, I noticed wooden frames covered with metal mesh with a hole in the middle. They explained to me that in each of them, a tree had been planted and there was a guard who watered them as they did in the other plantations. The idea was to stabilize the dunes to reduce the dust clouds. But a strong storm once again got the best of man. The wind had blown the small trees away and of course the dune was gone, leaving behind only the wooded frame. The experiment had been a total failure, hence retaining a sand dune against the onslaught of the wind proved to be a completely futile idea.

Early the next morning, we made our way back to Ulaanbaatar but by road this time. We drove through the desert in the middle of nowhere and our driver continued to amaze me by choosing from time to time to go either left or right. I was hoping that he knew where he was going. I had no choice as I had to trust him anyway. My Mongolian friends who were accompanying me seemed to be quite confident, which reassured me. The tracks left by the vehicles formed lines with strange shapes in the desert sand. When the road was too bumpy, the driver simply left the road to drive beside the tracks, which probably created a new parallel road. We travelled this way for nearly five hundred kilometres, while being shaken in the small van all the way. This was a Russian van, with simple mechanics that allowed it to start up with a crank. Two large fuel tanks gave it the required autonomy for this type of expedition. Comfort was very average and when we arrived in the capital in the early evening after a very long day, I ended up with a stomach ache after having been shaken for so many hours. That evening, I had a quiet dinner in the hotel's dining room before going to bed, because the next day we had to leave in a different direction to visit another project.

The next day, we headed east toward Karakorum in the province of Örvökhangaï. The road was paved, but the holes were so wide and deep that it was faster to ride in the desert next to the road. It looked like the road had been bombed over its entire length. You can easily imagine that the journey was rather painful. Next, we visited another tree project and once again we slept in a tourist camp. Since we were more north, it got a little colder and in the morning, at dawn, it was a great pleasure to see a young employee from the camp come into our yurt to start a fire in our stove. This meant that we could get up and get dressed in comfort even though our clothes had not yet had time to warm up.

The day before, I had been invited to go see the stars. Three of us drove a few kilometres from the camp near a river and we laid down on the ground to watch the Milky Way. I never imagined that there were so many stars in the sky! Away from the bright city lights, in the desert, under a clear sky, the show was absolutely gorgeous. I had never seen anything like it. What a sight! Of course, I had the opportunity to look at the sky while I was in the forest, but it never appeared so bright. With the sound of the river and the beautiful view we had of the Milky Way, this moment was magical for me and was added to my list of best memories of the trip.

The next day, on our way back we stopped near the city of Karakorum to visit the Erdene Zuu Buddhist monastery which had been built in 1585. As we got closer, we saw a huge enclosure that surrounded a group of buildings which formed an impressive wall with one hundred and eight stupas that stood around the place. These were small white temples, square at the base and topped by a conical shape which in turn was topped with a small mast to store relics. These stupas gave the enclosure an image of solidity and grandeur. Monks were still living in the monastery and I was impressed to see them with minimal clothing, wearing only their traditional saffron-coloured costume, characteristic of Buddhist monks. The weather was cool this morning and I was glad that I had my wool sweater and my windbreaker.

The Erdene Zuu temple is the oldest Tibetan Buddhist temple in Mongolia and is now part of the world cultural heritage. Its extensive enclosure contains sixty-two complete temples. All this, which could be seen from the top of a nearby hill that stands out in the desert with its vaulted walls and the white stupas.

There were more surprises in store for me on the road back to Ulaanbaatar. One of the Rotarians, who was accompanying us, asked our driver to stop at the next nomadic yurt that he saw along the road. He said that he wanted to pick up some camel milk, because it had been a long time since he had tasted any. Our driver stopped at a group of three yurts set up a few hundred metres from the road. Since you can drive just about anywhere through the desert, he drove right up to these yurts. Our friend then got out to meet the nomadic family and when he came back several minutes later he told us that these people had invited us into their yurt.

The Family Yurt

So, we got out of the car and the group headed over to the family waiting for us at the door of the yurt. Our friend explained that the day before had been a Mongolian day of celebration equivalent to Thanksgiving at home. For them, receiving visitors was a good omen for the coming year, especially a visitor coming from as far away as me. I could only hope that they were right. They invited us inside the family yurt and I was assigned an honorary seat next to the father. The yurt was modestly furnished and some beds were arranged around the single circular room in the centre of which there was a small wood stove. This was quite a difference from the tourist yurt I had visited in Ulaanbaatar on my first day.

A large metal container filled with camel milk at room temperature was placed before me. Next, the father took a ladle and poured a good amount in a bowl which he then offered to me. Honestly, I simply hate milk at room temperature. I glanced over to my friends who were waiting to see how I would react. Seeing my hesitation a group member said in English: "Paul, you have no choice... it's hospitality."

I then made up a little white lie. I asked my friends to explain to this man that I did not usually drink milk because it gave me a stomach ache, but that I was still going to taste it to make them happy. So, I brought the bowl up to my mouth into which I dipped my shut lips and hoped that they would not notice my trick. I put the bowl down on the table in front of me and then they brought out a dish of goat meat. The dish was filled with chunks of meat that had been cut from the bone with a knife. The meat still had all its fat and I tried to take the piece with the least fat. The meat was very good and since I love goat meat, it was not difficult for me to polish it off. However, I kept the fat part in my hand until we actually left. I then gave the family dog a treat.

This visit made me realise the great similarities between these nomadic people and the Inuit of Northern Canada. Both are nomadic and live in round houses. Their food is very rich and fatty meat is part of their diet. Their lifestyle is similar. Their living conditions are difficult and life for them is tough. It is interesting to note the similarities as they live in two different areas of the world, far apart from each other and without communication between them. An anthropologist could explain this better than me.

A little further down the road we stopped once more, this time at a school built near a village. The school was a boarding school for nomadic children who spent time in the desert to graze their cattle. We were offered crackers, cheese and tea as a snack. But not just any tea! Grey tea made from tea and camel milk. The gray mixture was not appealing at all. It was accompanied by cubes of sugar that we put in our mouth to improve the taste! Since I do not drink tea, I politely refused explaining that I did not drink tea, which was true. Again, I had managed to get away with it...

After our snack, we were led into the large three-story building nearby. Upon entering, I saw young people in groups of four studying, each sitting at a small desk. It was very silent. There were children of all ages, from five or six years to twelve years. There reigned a calm that surprised me. One of the teachers showed us around the building, which was in poor condition. The woman explained that in winter they sometimes put all children in the same classroom to stay warm... My fellow Rotarians considered starting a project to change the windows of the building and provide a little more comfort to those children.

Truly Public Toilets

Back on the road, we stopped to refuel. I asked where the bathroom was and they pointed to an area a distance away from the gas station. Upon arrival, I realise that these toilets were just a big hole with a roof and walls on three sides. Two large planks served as a floor and to complete your business, you had to go the back of the room. Not very inviting, especially with the smell, but when you got to go, you take whatever is available! So I sat down, dropped my pants and immediately realised I was directly across the road that brought us here. There was no door, and to ensure privacy, three horizontal boards formed a small fence of less than one metre in height in front of the shelter to "protect" users from being seen by cars passing by. Although there was very little traffic on this road, a car appeared at a time when I was really busy! I hurried to finish my task and join the group. Looking back, I still laugh at this funny incident and still wonder who could have installed a toilet in a place like this?

We then continued our journey to the capital, where I spent my last night in this country. My flight was at half past eight in the morning and we agreed that I would be picked up at about six thirty. As of 6:15 am I was in the hotel lobby having breakfast and waiting for my friends. Time flies and they only arrived at half past seven, one hour before my flight. I was getting really worried knowing that we needed to be at the airport well in advance, especially for international flights.

As we approached the airport, the driver of the van took the path that leads to the lower level of arrivals instead of heading to the path leading to departures. He passed the terminal without stopping. I watched him intently as I realised he was heading straight to the tarmac, to the same door we had taken when I arrived. Above the door, there was a poster I had not seen when I arrived and that simply said "VIP entrance".

I owe this special treatment to my friend Erdene, who had, in the past, occupied an important position in the Ministry of Interior of Mongolia. He had classified visitors from Rotary International as VIP guests of Mongolia. Today, Erdene holds a position at the Delegation of Mongolia at the United Nations.

We were greeted by a policeman who asked me for my tickets. He asked which suitcases were mine. After confirming that I was leaving for Quebec via Moscow, Paris and Montreal, a young attendant invited me to the VIP lounge with my friends. She returned ten minutes later and gave me my boarding passes for Quebec, which surprised me as I was travelling with three different companies: Aeroflot to Moscow, Air France from Moscow to Paris and Montreal and Air Canada to Quebec City.

My friends and I enjoyed these last moments together. They then gave me a memento of my visit to Mongolia, a musical instrument called a "horse-head violin." It is a three-stringed instrument with a soundboard; it is square and the headstock is beautifully carved in the shape of a horse's head. I was delighted to receive this exceptional piece. This violin now has a special place in my home. I was still thanking my friends for their present when the attendant approached and said, "Mr. Beaulieu, the airplane is ready, all that's missing is you!"

One last goodbye to my friends and I followed the attendant through the corridors of the airport that lead directly to the boarding gate. Arriving near the plane, my hand luggage was passed through an x-ray machine. It was the only security formality with which I had to comply. I had not seen the inside of the Ulaanbaatar airport. I rushed onto the plane and realised that I had been upgraded to business class. Arriving in Quebec after thirty-six hours of travel, I found my bag with a big red sticker that read "Mongolian Airlines VIP". Without a doubt, in Mongolia, VIPs are truly entitled to a very special treatment!

INDIA

Train Tickets Please!

The taxi driver turned onto a narrow street crowded with vehicles and people. It was eleven o'clock local time. After a long thirty-four hour trip, taking into account the waiting time in the airport, we finally arrived at our hotel. We were in the heart of Delhi, India. Since we were totally exhausted, we quickly went to our rooms to rest for a few hours, because the next day we had to take the train at seven forty to go to Chandigarh, a city located two hundred and sixty kilometres further north, to meet our contact.

I was in India along with Serge Poulin who had asked me to accompany him. He was getting ready to become the next District Governor of Rotary International and was planning a development project in the region. Given our respective obligations, this trip would be very short, as a matter of fact way too short! But we had no choice because we wanted to visit the project site before getting involved in this adventure. With the experience I had gained over the years, I learned that it is always good to know who we are dealing with before undertaking a major project. Many difficulties are avoided and this ensures that the odds are on our side for the project to be completed. Before Serge and I decided to come see things first hand, I had exchanged many emails with Navjit.

After a night cut short, we were ready to hit the road to Chandigarh. The hotel porter showed us a rickshaw, which is a bicycle with a seat for two passengers located behind the driver. As the train station was very close, we were told that this was the best way to get there. Both bags were mounted on the support behind our seat, and off we went to the railway station. Our driver struggled to start moving because of our weight and that of our two suitcases.

Daylight was upon us and everything seemed different: the noise, the traffic and people everywhere, not to mention the pervasive smoke of charcoal produced by the food counters lining the streets. The hotel porter informed us that the journey would cost thirty rupees, but at the station, our driver asked us for fifty rupees each! It is not the price that shocked us, but the fact that he tried to take advantage of us. Fifty rupees is the equivalent to $1.10 Canadian and his effort was well worth it. We agreed to fifty rupees for both and this is how our adventure began!

We crossed the street and entered the station carrying our suitcases. The floor was covered with people lying everywhere bundled up as best they could to deal with the rather cool morning. We stopped to check the name of the train posted on our tickets as all the trains have names in India. Ours was called Kalka Shtbdi. Fortunately, it also had the number 12011!

A man posted in front of the doors that led to the train boarding platforms saw us and asked if we needed help. I showed him the document that I had in my hand and he informed me that it was not valid to board the train. It was only a reservation and not a ticket! Yet I had bought this ticket before departure.

He explained in broken English that we had to go to a sales office. He tried to show us a big building where the office was located. Since we did not seem to understand his explanations, he then asked us to follow him. We took our luggage and followed him to where the motorized rickshaws waited for their customers. He explained to the rickshaw driver that he had to take us to the ticket office. So we found ourselves in traffic again with our driver trying to get out of the traffic jam around the station.

Our Good Samaritan from the station had told us that the office was very close, but our rickshaw driver turned onto a large boulevard and seemed determined to go much farther than originally mentioned. Serge and I looked at each other and asked ourselves if we were being ripped off! After about two kilometres, the driver dropped us off in front of a building with a sign that read "Train Tickets". Relieved, we followed him inside, aware of the little time we had. Our train was leaving in ten minutes and we still did not have our tickets!

It became obvious that we would not be able to get back to the station before the train left. The time needed for the formalities and the trip back to the station would take at least a good fifteen minutes, so we had to find another solution.

The person at the ticket office suggested a taxi. He made us a first offer of almost $300 to get us to Chandigarh. He explained that this was a luxury car and well worth the price. This was definitely too expensive and our driver made two more offers which were rejected before we finally agreed on a price of $120, which was significantly better than his first offer. It felt like a well prepared tourist trap, but we had to get to our destination as soon as possible because we had an invitation to attend a wedding in the evening. Moreover, Navjit Singh Aulakh would be waiting for us at the train station around eleven o'clock.

Our driver arrived. His name is Bente and he was wearing a turban since he was a Sikh. He spoke acceptable English and we sat in the back seat of his little car for the trip to Chandigarh. We arrived around one o'clock, after more than five long hours of driving. During the trip, we had the opportunity to appreciate the infernal traffic in India and we were pleased that Serge and I did not have to drive!

On the highway, the two lanes were shared between motorcycles, tractors, trucks and even rickshaws, especially when we got closer to the cities. Every time we went through a city, we were astonished. Intersections were incredibly crowded and everyone tried to squeeze into even the smallest hole that would allow them to move ahead. Here everyone drives by honking: one honk to say "I am here", another to inform others that we are changing lanes, yet another one to urge the car in front of us to go a little faster. The result is a concert of cars honking their horns which is actually quite amazing. Trying to understand how they manage to avoid accidents is quite an achievement. Vehicles brush each other, crisscross and cut each other off in an amazing synchronicity. Our driver was careful and we managed to arrive safely at our hotel.

It is unusual for this kind of trip to be booked in a five-star hotel. Not everyone is welcome and, needless to say, security is tight. When we arrived at the gate, security guards opened the hood of the car and inspected the underside of the vehicle with a mirror before finally opening our doors wide to provide access to the hotel courtyard. Before going inside, we had to put our bags through a metal detector and of course we also had to go through just like we did in airports! At least we would be able to sleep knowing we were safe!

Navjit had scheduled an appointment for four o'clock at our hotel so this gave us time to eat, get some rest and unpack. We were already in the lobby when he arrived. We were finally able to meet the person with whom we had exchanged so many emails in recent months.

Navjit is a Sikh and he wears a turban. He's a friendly chap, an engineer by profession, but he does not seem to fit the typical image of engineers. On his Facebook page, he posts almost daily thoughts, inspiring images and reflections on life. I can say he is not very Cartesian as engineers usually are.

He made an appointment with Dr. Jatinder, an ophthalmologist who runs the JP Eye Hospital, a hospital for eyes. Dr. Jatinder Shingh agreed to meet us on a Sunday afternoon during a long weekend off. Dr. Shingh, who received us, conducts "camps for eyesight" twenty times a year. In these camps, Dr. Shingh and his colleagues operate on hundreds of people with cataracts, and they do this free of charge. Serge Poulin, who was accompanying me, is an optician by profession and he is always interested in problems concerning vision. During his year as District Governor, he wanted the project for our district to deal with this health aspect.

Dr. Shingh showed us around his "hospital" which is more like a clinic as we know in America. Two of his young assistant ophthalmologists were also present during the visit. They are very committed people who did not hesitate to take the time to meet with us during their day off. Serge and the ophthalmologist seemed to understand each other in their technical language when they spoke together concerning the "camps for eyesight." A financial project is currently being developed so that we can help the doctor operate on about two thousand people. Each eye operation costs about USD $33. The only thing left to do is to purchase the medical equipment since all the work is done by volunteers.

After this very informative visit, Navjit and his driver took us to our hotel and we agreed to meet at 8:30 pm at another hotel where we were invited to attend the wedding of the daughter of one of his best friends. Of course, Serge and I were delighted with the invitation and we were very much looking forward to attending the wedding. For us, this would be a privileged contact with the local culture and customs.

A Hindu Wedding

Around nine o'clock, Serge and I arrived at the hotel where the wedding was to take place. Navjit welcomed us and showed us to our table where we could clearly see the married couple. The great room was half full and the servers were quick to put dishes garnished with appetizers of all kinds before us. I had never seen so many servers in a reception hall in all my life. Every thirty seconds someone offered us either food or something to drink. I noticed that no alcoholic beverages were served. We were told with a smile that young people often go outside... Who knows why! We were quickly surrounded by girls about ten years old who were curious to see these two strangers. One of them who was especially outgoing spoke English and before we knew it we were bombarded with questions like: Where do we come from? Why we are here, if we like the food, etc. Afterward we decided to take pictures of them. They laughed and of course the fun continued and then someone introduced a couple to the table who were friends of the family. He was Greek and she was Ukrainian, a tall woman with golden blonde hair that quickly attracted the young girls who proceeded to bombard her their interrogations.

We were informed that the groom had arrived so we followed the crowd outside to meet him in the parking lot. The crowd walked toward the parking lot entrance where sounds of drums and shouts of joy could be heard. I tried to find a spot to see what was happening when I noticed the crowd gathering around what seemed to be the bride arriving on a donkey. I could not see her face as she was wearing a hat decorated with stones and wrapped in long pearl tassels. The happy procession moved very slowly, as the crowd danced at the sound of the drums. Interestingly enough, the group kept stopping and it would take them nearly an hour to reach the entrance of the building which was located less than thirty feet away.

What a surprise to find out that it was not the bride, but the groom! I had never seen a groom dressed that way! His hat richly decorated and his embroidered garments had tricked me into believing that this was the bride. I realised my mistake only when he lifted the long pearl tassels that hid his face. Before going inside, the crowd stopped once more and now it was the groom's family's turn to offer gifts to the bride's family to mark the union of families. All this took place in a very festive atmosphere without established protocol and everyone was given hugs.

After all the celebrations, the groom finally made his entrance into the room and headed slowly toward the platform adorned with a double sofa covered with red satin. He was accompanied by his friends who had been following him since his arrival. When he managed to climb up onto the stage, the photo-shooting started. All this was filmed by two camera crews accompanied by a host of amateur photographers, including me.

Noise coming from outside of the room told us that it was time for the bride to come in. I saw a canopy decorated with flowers. I started moving closer with the rest of the guests to see the bride and her mother who were moving slowly. She was wearing a red dress embroidered with pearls and her head was covered with a scarf. On her forehead, a jewel was secured by an embroidered headband with red pearls hanging down. From this headband, a small chain covered with jewels hung from her forehead and it was clipped to her nostrils. She was a true princess of the Arabian Nights! Her father joined them and accompanied them to the stage where the bride joined her future husband.

A crowd once again rushed around the stage, so I could not see what was going on. I was later told that a short ceremony was conducted upon the arrival of the bride, but it must have been very short, because I did not get to see anything! After a few moments, the couple finally met and then another long photo session began. Everyone present in the room was photographed in turn with the newlyweds. All the while, disco music was being played and soon the teenagers invaded the dance floor. A huge buffet was then served: the tables were aligned along three walls of the room. Four hundred guests lined up at the countless dishes that gave off a fantastic smell, each one just as pleasant as the next one. Most of them were vegetarian, but there were some dishes with lamb and they were absolutely delicious!

The meal ended after midnight; and it was time for Serge and I to go back to our hotel. We were told that the party would continue into the wee hours of the morning, but this was way too much for us. It had been a long day and the previous night had been too short. Before leaving, Navjit told us that he would join us at our hotel around half past eleven, which would give us time to recover a bit and relax before getting back to work. Finally, we thanked our hosts before jumping into a taxi.

Water, Toilets and Cataract Operations!

Our friend picked us up around noon. He appeared to be in good shape even though he had gone to bed much later than us. We headed out to visit various projects that clubs in the region supported in Chandigarh. We began by visiting a poor neighbourhood where a health centre was located which included a computer training centre for disadvantaged youth. On our way there we saw a slum like the one made famous by the film Slumdog Millionaire by Danny Boyle.

We noticed it from far away and I was unable to take pictures because of the distance. As is often the case when travelling, once you've missed the opportunity to view or purchase something, rarely does the opportunity repeat itself. This proved to be true as throughout our trip we would not see this kind of slum again. We were in the north of India where there is less poverty than in the south.

One of the projects we wanted to undertake was the distribution of water purifiers in homes. As we wanted to see what the purifiers looked like, Navjit asked his driver if he would take us to his home, because he had one. He agreed and we ended up in the driver's house located in a popular area. This was not a poor neighbourhood, but rather a neighborhood of workers. The apartment was small and we were told that the living room was also used as a bedroom. His mother and brother also lived in the apartment with him and his wife. The building was made of cement and so were the walls and the floor. Everything was gray. He showed us the water filter while his mother prepared tea and biscuits: Indian hospitality at its best!

Navjit and his driver then took us to the Rotary House. This building contained a meeting room for the Chandigarh club and the district governor's office. This office was opened by a Canadian named Wilfred Wilkinson during his year as president of Rotary International in 2007-2008. The building was impressive and I wished that we could have the same thing here. However, I understand that the money that we do not invest in such equipment is used for the benefit of the people from the community.

After a hearty meal at the restaurant, we continued on to visit other projects by Rotarians, including a huge blood collection centre. Obviously, clubs in the area appeared to have impressive resources!

Back at the hotel, we had an appointment with Manmohan Singh, the elected governor of the district; it is with him we would be pursuing our goals. The meeting took place in the early evening with his two sons who are his pride and joy, and rightly so, because they are two bright young men and they are very well educated. Even though the father wears a turban, the sons decided not to follow suit. Manmohan told us that this was a personal choice and that they were free to make that decision. We then went to a restaurant for dinner where Navjit joined us. We went back to the hotel early because of the ten-hour time difference, which was hard on us.

The next morning, Manmohan's driver picked us up at our hotel to take us to a small town located about an hour's drive from Chandigarh. Traffic was intense. Once there, we saw Manmohan coming toward us dodging between cars and crowds. He welcomed us with the presidents of two other Rotary Clubs. They showed us a few projects they had completed, but especially the places dealing with public latrine projects that we planned to support. For Rotarians, water and latrines are two inseparable elements to improving health in developing countries.

After dining at the restaurant with three club presidents, they had us visit an orphanage and it was an opportunity for us to participate in the distribution of blankets for the orphans. The orphanage had about twenty boys who came from the streets. Orphans enjoyed a minimum comfort, but at least they were safe, had enough food and were able to go to school. The orphanage was funded essentially by one of the club presidents who joined us. He wore a turban and a long white and wide beard; I must say he looked like a good father. We could see his generosity on his face but the difference in language prevented us from communicating with him properly.

When the orphans arrived from school, one after the other, they came to greet us by touching our knees. This was a form of respect for them, but I also think one of submission. I did not ask too many questions regarding this custom even though it bothered me because I did not want to make my guests uncomfortable. I could not change this habit anyway!

Back in Chandigarh, before leaving for Delhi, we had coffee and our friend Navjit joined us and governor-elected Manmohan to discuss the administrative part of the projects. We had to take the six o'clock train to get back to Delhi. We left Navjit at the restaurant and Manmohan accompanied us to the train station.

He took us to the boarding platform and waited with us until the train arrived. He made sure that we were well settled in before leaving. The train left the station and during the whole three hours we were served a delicious five-course meal! We had second class seats, what they call third class, but it didn't matter, because I really did not understand their system. I guess that first class must have been even better. We settled in very comfortably and we took this time to relax a bit and talk about what we had seen. Arriving at our hotel in Delhi, we checked in and verified the validity of our train tickets with the front-desk clerk, because the next day we were leaving for Agra to visit one of the Seven Wonders of the World, the Taj Mahal.

From Misery to the Taj Mahal

We left the hotel early in a rickshaw to reach the station on time. Again, we made our way through the people lying on the floor and we arrived at the station platform. We tried to find the name and number of our train, but after going through several gateways to find the pier where our train was to leave, we decided to ask at a coffee counter. The employee did not speak English and we could not understand him. Then another customer came along, a young man who spoke English. Looking at our tickets, he told us that we are not at the right station! The station where we were to catch our train was twenty minutes away and our train left in fifteen minutes!!!

Obviously, using the train system in India was not our cup of tea! Upon leaving the station to go buy other tickets, someone showed us the Ticket Office located in front of the station. We realised at that moment that three days earlier we could have gotten tickets at this office which would have given is the time to take the train to Chandigarh. There was no need to go as far as we did. We had actually been conned royally. But that's part of the travelling experience. We learn how things work and the next time we visit, we avoid these pitfalls.

In this travel office, after realising that all the trains were full, again we were offered to go there by taxi! We negotiated and agreed on a price that included the taxi, the guide at the Taj Mahal and the entrance fee. As the price was reasonable for us, but probably too expensive anyway, we decided to accept this offer and go to Agra whatever the cost because we only had this one day to see this wonder of the world.

Our driver was a man in his thirties. From the start, we realised that he drove fast and he was an expert in slalom as he passed cars in an incredible way. He knew perfectly well the dimensions of his vehicle. Every time I thought he would have an accident, he somehow managed to get through. Of course, like everyone else, his driving included a lot of honking. All the drivers here seemed to ignore the wonderful invention of flashers!

Upon arrival in Agra, the traffic was heavy. Since we had a driver who knew the city well, he took a shortcut and then close to the Taj Mahal he made a short stop to pick up our guide. We found out that that this guide spoke French which was well appreciated. Serge and I wondered if we would be "wowed" or if this wonder of the world was overrated. Before entering the actual site of the Taj Mahal, we had to go through to metal detectors. There was one line for men and another one for women, because security guards were doing a tactile search. Finally, we met at the gate of the building.

The enclosure was surrounded by a high wall of red bricks. The portal consisted of a large red brick façade with white lines and flowers inlaid in marble. Right at the entrance, Quranic verses were calligraphed with inlaid black marble right at the entrance of the Taj Mahal itself. The portal was majestic and it must have been nearly thirty metres high. It was topped with twenty-two small domes which represented the years that it took to build the mausoleum. There was however no consensus on the exact duration of the construction, with some suggesting twelve years and others twenty-three years. Our guide spoke of twenty-two. After some explanations from our guide, we entered the enclosure and it is at this time that we were finally able to see the Taj Mahal!

We went through the hall gate which was a dark room made of red marble covered with inlays such as those we saw on the outside. Still we were unable to see the wonderful building itself. I listened to the explanations of our guide, which seemed endless because it was the Taj Mahal itself that I was looking forward to seeing. Finally, we got through the hall and headed for the door that gave us access to the object of our trip.

It was a beautiful day with bright sunshine. As soon as we arrived outside Serge and I looked at each other and said, "Wow!" What a splendor! Huge and impressive, the Taj Mahal stood before us and its bright white marble contrasted beautifully against the blue sky. The majestic building showed its perfect lines with its four minarets overlooking the esplanade. An imposing dome dominated everything in harmonious lines equally perfect. This was by far one of the most beautiful handmade buildings on earth. We were moving slowly to take in all the breathtaking beauty that surrounded us. It goes without saying that I took lots of pictures. The base of the building, which must be at least a dozen metres wide, gave the structure a look of immense stability and solidity.

The entrance arch was a true masterpiece in itself with its thirty-five metres of white marble. Reliefs carved directly in stone surrounded the entrance. In all, twenty-eight kinds of stones were used to perform the various inlays of the Taj Mahal. Honestly, a marvellous work of craftsmanship. The inlay of stones was made with such precision that it was impossible to distinguish the change in stone as we passed our hand over it. Absolutely stunning!

The Taj Mahal is a mausoleum built by the Mughal emperor Shan Jahan in memory of his wife Arjumand Banu Begam, also known as Mumtaz Mahal, which means "light of the palace" in Persian. She died in June 1631 and her inconsolable husband built this mausoleum to serve as the final resting place of her body. At his death in 1666 he was placed next to his wife.

When you enter the mausoleum, the room is dark because it is lit up by windows made up of small holes like those of a honeycomb. The woman's tomb stands at the centre of the large room under the central dome, while the Emperor is on her left. A corridor surrounds the mausoleum. We toured the building to admire all the details and then headed for the exit, but before leaving, I took one last photo from a viewpoint suggested to me by our guide: the Taj Mahal appearing in the centre of an arch. One last look and we left the enclosure.

We returned to Delhi where we spent our last day visiting and shopping for souvenirs. The previous day we had called our first driver, Bente, who had driven us to Chandigarh, so that he could show us around the city. He had us visit the Parliament buildings whose architecture is typical of the English who had dominated this country for many years. The streets in this area are wide. A long boulevard leads to the Parliament Buildings and this is where the grand parade for the national holiday is held annually.

Bente brought us to a few shops where I did some souvenir shopping while Serge took the opportunity to pack his bags with items that were to be sold during the silent auction at his district's conference. The funds thus raised would be added to the funds available for a fourth project that was to be developed in the field of education.

Before heading to the airport, Bente showed us a Bahia temple. The building was built in the shape of a lotus flower with the same white marble as that used to build the Taj Mahal. Due to time constraints we were not able visit it, but the building was absolutely beautiful. With this last image in mind, we left the country to go back home.

After this short stay in India, I understood better the attraction of this country. There is so much to discover. I'll have to go back one day...

8

WHAT'S LEFT?

After ten years of involvement in all these projects, I wanted to know how each of them had evolved. Were all those efforts and all that time invested really worth it? I sought information on the projects from those with whom I had occasional contacts as well as those with whom I had regular contacts and the results were very interesting.

Starting with the low-cost-shelter project in Brazil, we should keep in mind that the families who had received a house had to keep it five years before being able to sell it. Of course, after five years, a community life had been established and almost each and every family was still living in the same neighbourhood.

Jean-Hugues Laflamme, the District Governor who initiated the orphanage in Bacau, Romania, is still in touch with them and he continues to support and help them with his club by financing smaller projects that help them to respond to the various needs that arise from time to time. Jean-Hugues keeps up to date on the situation of the institution that he helped to build and which is close to his heart. I am sure he will keep an eye on it for the rest of his life. Nothing is more normal after having been involved in such a cause than wanting to keep abreast of the situation. Moreover, when we are the foster parent of this type of project, we want the benefits for the people to last for as long as possible.

The same thing applies to me when it comes to the Instituto Agropecuario in Peru. The Institute is working well and it actually offers two types of three-year courses where students can obtain a certificate as a "Food Industry Technician" or a "Technician for Food Production". In 2014, forty-three students got their diploma after three years of study and they were able to enter the job market. Local industries working in the food industries are now associated with the Institute and they even offer work sessions for the students

I don't know exactly how many students have graduated from the Institute since its inception but I am sure that those who have completed their courses have a better life and that goes for their families as well. Besides, with a diploma in their hands, they are more likely to find a better quality job.

The impact of such an Institute is hard to measure without doing an exhaustive study and a close follow-up with former students. However, we can easily imagine that many of them have found better paying jobs than if they had not had that training. When I see that private companies are involved, I think it is safe to say that the Institute has been meeting the need.

The next project was the water project in Cojimies. It has taken several years for this project to be completed. After all, we started its preparation in 2003 and the last part was only completed in 2011. In June of 2014, I had the opportunity to return so I could further plan for the addition of some other water systems in some remote areas of the village. Even though there are some maintenance and management problems, there is hope for the sustainability of the projects for the first time since 2003. I met with the mayor of the regional municipality of Pedernales. This new mayor really wants to be involved. Moreover, he now wants the municipality to supervise the water committees to make sure that the systems are well managed. I have to say that prior to having been involved in municipal politics the new mayor was an activist who was dedicated to environmental causes. Therefore, he was naturally a lot more sensitive to these questions than many other politicians.

The mayor even spent a day with George Murillo and me. George was the first chairman of the water committee in Cojimies, and today he is the deputy-mayor of Pedernales. We visited together some very remote areas of the village to meet with the population so that we could talk about the water system that was soon to be installed. It was music to my ears to hear the mayor talking about sustainable development and to explain to the population how important it was to have good maintenance of "their" system. He was asking them to make a commitment regarding the proper management of their new water system.

The following day, I spent time with the Cojimies village committee which also had a great interest in making sure that the water system worked well. We went to see what was going on in two neighbourhoods where the system was not functioning anymore and the reason for that was because the pumps had been stolen. That gave us the opportunity to find a solution that would allow the system to work without pumps. All that was needed was to simply put the water tanks a little higher on a cement base and let gravity move the water to the main pumping system which is well protected. So, no more pumps to be stolen and less electricity to pay!

During that trip, I also met with the Bahia de Caraquez Rotary Club which is closer than the one from Portoviejo with whom we have worked since 2003. This club will now be in charge of developing new water projects. As some members of the Bahia de Caraquez club run businesses in Pedernales, it will be easier for them to supervise the progress of the projects thus alleviating George's work.

I was surprised by the economic activity that the small village of Cojimies actually generated. Many new hotels were built along the road that we took to go from Pedernales to Cojimies and in return they provided jobs for many people which kept the economy rolling. Many small shops were now installed on the beach to fulfill the tourists' needs, many more than there were a few years ago.

Thanks to the new road, tourists were now able to discover these long beaches and the economy was much stronger, which of course made me happy. The mobilisation of the villagers around the water project has had a huge impact on their fight to get a good road with the end results being that the tourist industry now creates good jobs. A large part of the population now depends on this industry for their livelihood. Recently, I had the opportunity to see some photos of the Corvina Festival, a large fish that abounds in that region, and more than five thousand people had invaded Cojimies for these celebrations. None of this would have been possible ten years ago.

Seeing these changes, we can safely say that water is the basis of everything. Water has an influence on the health of the local population, on the quality of their lives and on the economy in general. When we see the example of Cojimies, I think that all these years of involvement in this village yielded results well beyond our wildest expectations. Not that all the credit belongs to us, but I still believe that the arrival of the water there is at the origin of many of these improvements. I have also realised that when we are involved for a longer time in a village, the impact of our actions is much more significant than if we only carry out a single project. It even manages to change the mindset of people who now believe in the future of their village.

The water project in Ecuador was followed by the Agrofuturo school project. Unfortunately, the agricultural school had to close since the EPSOL University which was supervising the project did not have the budget to continue. We have to understand that the new government of Ecuador has reformed the education system over the past years under the new President Raphael Correa. He has put a lot of energy into redesigning the education system with regard to the training of teachers and the quality of schools. New schools have been built, while some others have been renovated and the universities are now under the direct and close supervision of the State.

However, the government has accepted the training principles that exist under Agrofuturo and they still continue to train the farmers. Unfortunately, there is no practical training as there was under our project. I had the opportunity to go into three villages in the mountains to meet with former students as well as the mayors of the villages. I wanted to know if Agrofuturo had fulfilled its promises and if it had had an impact in the communities. The mayors confirmed that the students are still working and that they were using the techniques they had learned. In another village, I also talked with three young men who took the training course and who were actually exploiting their fields. They discovered that corn offered the best results for crops in the area. I was accompanied on that that trip by a teacher from EPSOL University who knows the villages where the students come from and she was happy to show me the corn fields that grew thanks to drip irrigation, a cultivation technology that the students had learned. When I left the area, I was convinced that Agrofuturo had been fruitful. The fact that the government had taken over was proof that Agrofuturo had done a good job and that the training had contributed to the sustainable development of the region. The techniques that were taught and that will be transmitted to other people in these villages, as well as the next generation, means that a new tradition in farming methods now exists in this area.

During these past fifteen years, we have financed numerous projects and I have the conviction that repeated actions in the same location have a greater impact in the long run even if the smaller projects are more effective at meeting real needs. The improvement of many elements in the same community brings about a feeling of pride and hope that things will improve. It is then that we see community leaders taking over as my friend George Murillo did in Cojimies.

9

TEN HUMANITARIAN TRAVELLER RULES

The vast majority of those who have never visited a poor country as volunteer, are disoriented when they arrive on site for the first time. Continually confronted to their own values they are often destabilised. On a few of my trips I was joined by friends and acquaintances who wanted to live that experience. Almost each time, I had to intervene to put things into context.

One day, I was travelling with a group of friends who were accompanying me to Cojimies, the small village in Ecuador where we had managed to set up a water project. While visiting the poorest part of the village, as soon as they saw the wooden huts in which part of the population lived, I was asked why we were not building new houses instead of a water system.

The person who asked that question has always been interested in the real estate market. She has moved many times to improve the quality of her house and I have nothing against that but in a poor country the simple fact of having a house is a feat in itself. We always have to examine the priorities of the people who live in these houses before judging them based on our own values. We have to learn to question ourselves on why things are like that and to never try to judge with our North American eyes.

In that village, we have to remember ninety five per cent of the kids were sick because of the poor water quality. Therefore, these people had asked for clean water before anything else. To see our children perennially sick is a form suffering for any parent no matter what their level of living is. Having children in good health is a priority for any parent in this world whether rich or poor. Access to clean water is unfortunately a luxury for a large part of the population living on this planet.

That lady who was travelling with me for the first time had to change her way of looking at things. Her values were very different from the needs of these villagers and that is not the only thing that we have to adjust when we arrive in a place like this for the first time.

To help you to prepare for a stay in a developing country and to make sure that your trip is successful, the next pages will explain some basic rules. A successful trip will give you the desire to travel again and to live through new enriching experiences.

Rule #1: Too much could be hard!

A friend with whom I was talking to about my experiences abroad told me that she was thinking of going to a poor country when she retires. She explained that she wanted to leave for six to nine months. It is a very nice goal however the only problem is that she has never set foot in a developing country except during her annual vacation on the beach in the Caribbean.

There is a huge difference between a trip that we take as tourists, with nice accommodations in a four- or five-star hotel, and a humanitarian trip where most of the time we are very far from big cities and the comfort that we are used to. For the non-initiated person, the lack of comfort, the minimal sanitary facilities and the different food are such that he or she could easily and quickly find the situation difficult, not to say very painful.

For a first humanitarian trip, I suggest a short stay of one or two weeks. Even though you find the situation difficult to live through, you can put up with it two weeks, unless you get sick and the situation becomes unbearable.

We must also realise that as we get older, we are more attached to our comfort and our habits. So, it is better to check our capacity for adaptation before getting involved for a long-term project. Of course, this is different for each of us. Here, I will make an exception for young people looking for adventure. When we are young, we generally have a greater capacity to adapt and we find it easier to tolerate difficult living conditions. To sleep on a small mattress on the ground at the age of eighteen is not the same experience when we are over sixty!

If your first trip is a success, you will want to repeat the experience. On the contrary, if you are gone too long and find the experience difficult, then your career as a humanitarian worker will be short lived. So, it's better to put the odds in your favour in order to have a first successful trip.

Rule #2: Check the size of your bubble!

Each of us has our own bubble, which is the minimum space we need in order to be comfortable. Certain people have a larger bubble than others and have a hard time living in close proximity to their fellow human beings. In some countries, people are continuously touching each other. In North America, it is very different: when we touch another person inadvertently, we immediately hasten to apologize!

During one of my trips, my wife Aline who loves children, was being checked over by girls who seemed very attracted to her hair. She had brown hair with some blonde highlights. The young girls, all with very dark hair, wanted to touch hers. So, Aline sat on the sidewalk and let the girls touch her hair so they could see how it was possible for a person to have two colours in their hair! The children were touching her hair one after the other and they were laughing.

A friend who was with us watching the scene looked bewildered. She later admitted that she would be absolutely unable let the children touch her hair like that. When Aline and I were walking in the village, lots of kids followed us everywhere. They surrounded us and held our hands. The same friend then asked us how we could endure this since their hands were dirty!

As you can see, if you never had to test the size of your bubble, you just might have to deal with some surprising reactions when you are placed in such situations. It is better to know what to expect before leaving! Being better prepared, you will be able to control your reactions more easily.

Rule #3: Learn to say Good Day and Thank You!

Saying hello and thank you, is common courtesy. But to say it in the language of the inhabitants of the country where we are is a mark of respect even if we don't speak the language. How many times have I seen travellers unable to say thank you in the language of the country. Learning to say "gracias", "obrigado" or "spasiba" before leaving is not a difficult task.

At the beginning of the nineties, Aline and I had the opportunity to visit Russia. It was just after Perestroika. Before leaving we learned those two magical words: "spasiba" and "zdravsouitie". Thank you and Hello. It is incredible how those two small words, pronounced with a smile and an accent, were pleasing to the Russians.

In Spain, I saw a group of Australians who had been waiting for quite a long time before being able to make themselves understood that they simply wanted a beer. If they had a simple little pocket dictionary or a traveller's lexicon they would have avoided that disagreement. I was sitting beside them and even though I speak English and Spanish, I let them do things by themselves. I found them so unprepared for not having taken the elementary means to be able to make themselves understood that, quite frankly, I believe they simply deserved what was happening to them. We arrived only a few minutes before them but when we left after a hearty four-course meal with a nice bottle of Spanish wine, the Australians had still not been served their meal.

It is not mandatory to speak the language of the country but making a little effort will make your life easier. When you go to do humanitarian work, the same rule applies. Even if we don't speak the language, we need to be ready to make the required efforts to be understood and to communicate with the people. When we are able to say a few words to be understood and with the addition of body language and a nice smile, we break down barriers and open the way to communication.

Rule #4: Grumpy, beware!

There is no better opportunity to criticize than when we are travelling! At the end of the sixties, a friend of mine went to France as a tourist and came back with this comment about the Chateau de Versailles: "We had heard about that castle for years… It is not that extraordinary. These people didn't even have a toilet at that time and didn't wash themselves very often!"

As the saying goes: "Other times, other customs" We can also say "Other country, other customs!" No, it is not like back home. Elsewhere things are done differently and we have to accept that. Even the fact of doing things that appear to us to be completely inappropriate have their reasons and we have to accept that without criticizing.

I repeat: It is not because we live in a developed country that we have the monopoly on the truth. We have all been influenced by our history and customs. Some have adopted a different lifestyle from ours and it is not something to be automatically considered as bad. It is up to us to learn to live differently and this makes travelling an interesting experience. We also have to try to understand why things are done the way they are and this is how to learn more about the culture and lifestyle of our hosts. Keep an open mind and keep your thoughts to yourself, your new friends will really appreciate it.

So, if you're the type to criticize anything that is different, this kind of trip is not for you.

Rule #5: Food security

When talking about food security, we are generally talking about having access to food sources needed to feed all the country's people. But as a traveller, I am talking here about the way to feed yourself in a secure manner.

Despite the numerous trips that I have taken to all kinds of countries, I can tell you that I have never been sick, except for indigestion due to fatigue. I have to say that I am very cautious. Being sick while travelling is an experience you absolutely want to avoid. Take the advice of experienced travellers before leaving. This will protect you against gastronomic problems and also prevent you from experiencing some very bad moments.

It happened to me many times, especially in Africa, where I had to stop in a small restaurant along the road. When I was not sure about the quality of the food and the hygiene of the restaurant, I resorted to my favourite food choice: a baguette and a nice cold beer! The bread is always fresh and has been cooked. The beer is done with purified water and therefore it is safe to drink. Combined, they represent a nutritious meal which allows you to wait until the next meal. Always choose cooked food, avoid raw food even if it has been washed, such as salads, fruits and vegetables. Fruits that you peel yourself are usually safe.

If you still suffer from diarrhea, start eating food such as white rice. You will get back on your feet very soon. You have to avoid all dairy products. Do not act like a member of a group that came with me to Ecuador, and who had been sick. One day later, when our bus stopped at a gas station with a small store, I heard him telling his wife "Look, they have some ice cream. That will be good in this heat!" I could not hold back and I told him: "Don't touch that!" The words just came out! We still had eight hours to go on the bus and everyone was eager to get to destination, so I did not want to have a complicated trip

I use a small trick. Before leaving home, I buy nuts in bulk and I split them up into small plastic bags. Each morning I take one or two of these small bags and put them in my pocket. A handful of nuts keep our stomach content and as they are rich in protein, they tide us over for longer periods of time before our next meal.

Rule #6: Learn how to adapt or stay home!

Travelling in a developing country requires a huge capacity of adaptation. If you like well-planned trips and ones that are well organised, then this kind of trip is not for you. During trips to a developing country, nothing is more constant than change and we have to be ready for unforeseen changes at any given moment.

First, time management for people from southern countries is not the same as that for northern people. That is well known, but when we have to deal with that difference we also have to cope with it. In South America, I used to ask my friends if the planned meeting was on local time or on Canada time. Canada time meant to be on time. It was our daily joke. Done with a smile, this question always brought funny comments on this difference in our cultures.

Things are also organised differently. In India, even if I had reserved my train tickets before leaving, nothing worked except for the only journey that had been reserved by our hosts. In each case, we had to find a solution very quickly. Each time we had to find a taxi ready to do the trip and, most of all, find a chauffeur that knew the city and who could also get us to our destination. In addition, we had to negotiate the price for the trip even if we knew we were paying way too much, but that is part of the game. We have to be able to adapt very quickly to these changes and find good solutions without losing our smile.

Sometimes, even our own airlines play tricks on us. For that reason we also have to plan for delays so that we have enough time between our stops, have a telephone number on hand or an email address to warn those waiting for us about our delay. Once, it took me twenty-four hours more to get to my destination after a long wait at U.S. customs that made me miss my connecting flight to South America.

At home during winter, there is always the possibility of a snowstorm that can upset our schedule. When I went to India, the day before I was supposed to leave, my travel friend Serge and I agreed to go to the airport at five in the morning to try and catch the first flight to New-York so we could be ahead of the snowstorm. The airline accepted to change our tickets at no cost since we were travelling with them all the way to Delhi. I can tell you that even if we had a twelve-hour wait in New-York which we found long, it was a lot less stressful than having to wait out the storm at home and having to change all our flights. We must therefore also expect the unexpected! That day, the flight we were normally supposed to take never took off. I was proud of our initiative that allowed us to complete our trip as it had been planned.

Rule #7: Different doesn't mean bad

To really enjoy your trip, you need to have an open mind and try to understand why things happen as they do. This may appear to be foolish, useless or badly done when we look at things with our North American eyes, but it is probably what is best for the local situation.

In an African village where we stopped for lunch, at the entrance of the place where we were to eat, there was a big bowl of water which was meant to wash our hands. We all washed our hands in the same bowl. After the meal and having cleaned up the leftover food, we put our dirty dishes in the same water. At first sight, that could appear to be a serious lack of hygiene; but when we stop to think for a moment, that village was desperately lacking clean water and that way of doing things allowed them to maximize the use of the same water by using it for different things. Here in North America, water is everywhere so that way of doing things would not be acceptable.

Also, some rituals stem from religious beliefs or come from a tradition that has been passed on from generation to generation. It is not up to us to criticize these choices or these ways of doing things. Above all, we must not make the mistake of thinking that the way we do things is the best...

Rule #8: An open mind is required!

I asked my old college friend Eric Beaulieu what he and his wife Hélène would consider to be the basic quality needed for someone who wants to live through the experience of being a volunteer in a foreign county – I asked him as they have the experience staying abroad a few weeks at a time as volunteer. Their answer did not surprise me at all: "You should be flexible enough to adapt to the way of life of the people who live in poverty and simplicity. We need to forget the North American mentality that tends to want to show them how we do it. You must have tolerance to deal with noise, heat, the mentality of "asi es la vida" (that's life), food, and culture in general. Good knowledge of the political regime is essential in order to avoid blunders... Basic knowledge of the language also makes trade easier... and above all, avoid pity!"

In a few sentences, Eric and Hélène summarized the gist of what to do when we want to be a volunteer worker abroad: have an open and flexible mind. Perhaps this is why so many people say they want to go and help abroad, but few actually do. Of course, all this comes in addition to the preparation and sacrifices we must make to embark on such an adventure.

Eric told me many times how they had lived during their stay in Central America. What they had gone through was not too different from what I had gone through during my many trips. The big difference is that they were spending many weeks at the same place which puts emphasis on all the irritants and of course makes things harder to bear.

Rule #9: To serve each other

Because they live in one of the most economically developed countries in the world, many think that they have the solution to everything. The first reflex is to do as we do at home, but it is not as simple as that. The inhabitants of other countries have priorities and needs that are different from ours. We must not take everything for granted, which puts us at risk of doing things that are not useful.

The choice has to come from the locals who know their needs and can explain them to us. This will make it easier for them to own the project, otherwise the work we do will not result in what we call sustainable development. As soon as we are gone, the project will fail because it will remain the foreigner's project and not theirs.

Besides that, this is why foreign aid has accomplished next to nothing for decades in many countries, because the projects or institutions that Westerners implemented have never become the people's own project. These initiatives did not meet their needs or values. That's why the large international non-governmental organisations dedicated to help developing countries have changed their approach in recent years.

We have to avoid going against this basic rule. A friend, Pierre Paré, who spends many long months each year in Guatemala describes this rule perfectly: "For a volunteer, it is very important to have the capacity to be able to serve the people you want to help, which means listening to them in order to respond to their needs, their expectations, which does not always coincide with the vision of people from the North. Often, Northerners arrive with some "ready to use" solutions in their mind, they have the resources, the know-how, the education and a lot of knowledge… we have to avoid making an exaggerated display of such thinking". We have to see where the people we want to help are in their own development, depending on the location and the timing of the help. Do they want the solution we are offering? Are they able to realise it, to take charge of it and to assure its sustainability? What will their contribution be? Will they be contributing to their project or only its beneficiaries?"

What Pierre is saying in short is that we must eat a little humble pie. Serving another person who is poorer, less educated and less wealthy is not given to everyone. Yet what Peter describes is an absolute truth.

When we go to foreign country to help, it is not to show our knowledge and our way of doing things. We have to use "their" way of doing things to provide them with what they need. It is as simple as that. Of course, in certain areas, we have some knowledge of technologies but we have to suggest rather than impose.

What struck me very often was the level of knowledge that southern populations have. What is missing most of the time is the financial means that allows them to apply it to their reality. We must keep in mind that we are only there to serve, as stated by my friend Pierre.

Rule #10: Do your homework before leaving!

Whoever wants to go abroad as a volunteer or to help the local population should do their homework before leaving. If we want our help to be effective, I suggest, for the first times, that you travel with a well-established organisation that is used to working in the country you are headed for and used to taking care of volunteers. You will then be better managed and will avoid unpleasant surprises. They will give you the training before you leave to get you ready for what you will experience on site.

Nothing is more troublesome for a person in charge of a group of volunteers abroad than to have to manage a badly prepared person. Often volunteers arrive fully motivated and with an abundance of good will but with a bad knowledge of what they are up against when in the field and how the things have to be done in the destination country.

They arrive with their cameras, their jewels, their fashionable clothes and their gifts. We should know that the more discreet we are, the more effective our actions will be. Giving gifts is okay but we have to give them with discretion and without ostentation. If you brought some material in great quantity, it is better to give it to a person in charge and let that person do the distribution. That person generally knows better who needs it the most. If you really have the desire to give, you don't need to publicise it and to inform the entire population. One of the mottos of Rotary International members is: "Service above self"! When we want to give I think we have to do it while forgetting our personal benefits.

Preparation involves a lot of small details. I will always remember a young lady who joined our group while we were going to a very poor area in Africa. She was the only one who travelled first class with the flight tickets her father gave her. Once she had arrived in Africa, she kept looking for automatic banking machines to get some money. Of course, she had a hard time finding these machines and she was a burden for the entire group because in each and every small town we went through with the bus, she would ask to stop at the bank to see if she would be able to withdraw some money with her bank card. Obviously, she knew very little about Africa when she decided to join the group for that trip.

Our group leader in Africa, my belated friend Bawa Mankoube, offered to lend her some money in local currency. She would be able to reimburse him as soon as we got back to Ouagadougou, the capital city of Burkina Faso, where we were going to take our flight back home. She refused Bawa's offer which upset him. To calm him down, I took him aside and explained the difference in the mentalities of our two countries. "Bawa, here you are used to saying that a whole village is needed to raise a child. You are used to putting all your resources in common and to helping each other out. At home, in the big apartment building where I live, I don't even know my neighbours. Therefore, for us it is unthinkable to even imagine we could borrow money in these conditions. It is not because that young lady does not trust you, it is only because she is not used to receiving help from her neighbours!"

That explanation appeared to have satisfied my friend Bawa. The other group members, all from North America, found the young lady's attitude perfectly logical. Once again, a great deal of discomfort was caused by ignorance.

Remember these ten rules when you are getting ready for your trip. They will help you avoid odd situations and your trip will be more agreeable. It is you who will benefit and who will come back with you head full of pleasant memories. Then maybe like me, you will be looking forward to leaving again for new horizons so you can live new experiences!

10

CONCLUSION

To Each His Own ....

I have always admired those who give their lives to help the needy. These tireless workers have my admiration, whether social workers, health care workers, or the many people who work in counseling. This is without forgetting those working for non-profit organisations; most of the time badly paid with meagre wages, but who have an incredible importance in the eyes of the poor. Our society could not function without them.

There are also all those who decide one day to quit everything to go and work as volunteers abroad. We are less aware of these individuals at home, because not only do they work behind the scene, but they are far from us and we hear very little about them. During my travels I met many of these dedicated persons who had to endure difficult living conditions to help the poor. Whether they are members of a religious community or development aid volunteers as they are sometimes called, these people have my admiration.

As many others, I would have loved to go abroad but when you have a wife and three children such a choice has a huge impact on the lives of your loved ones. Even more so, if like me you don't have a profession considered to be useful for working in a developing country, this makes things even more complicated. I do not see how my expertise could be useful, because nowhere have I seen a demand for a volunteer in financial planning! Nowhere either have I seen a request for people to work who can do nothing with their hands considering that there are a lot of skillful people in those countries. Thus the possibilities for me to be useful abroad were very thin. At least I was unable to see them.

As I told you at the beginning of this book, it was by being involved in my own community that I found the way to be useful abroad. By being active in the many Rotary International programs I was able to work at the international level.

There are many other organisations that could offer you the possibility to work as a volunteer in an activity connected to international aid. When we are involved in such an organisation working in foreign countries, it then becomes easier to discover the many possibilities that can open up for us.

Over the years, I have developed an expertise in the financing structures of humanitarian projects. At the same time, I have also developed an expertise in project monitoring and evaluation as well as in project stewardship. Being able to realise some projects is important but making sure they are well managed, that the money is well spent and is used for what it was intended is also very important. How many times have we heard horrible stories on the misuse of the money given to some organisations? Fortunately, the vast majority of our giving is well spent.

As many other non-governmental organisations, Rotary International with whom I am involved has set up an on-site verification system for the projects to make sure that the money will be well spent. Many volunteers give their time to go and evaluate the projects, check the books and make a report. A certain percentage of the project budget is planned for such verification costs. In doing so, the donors are sure that their money will be used for the right purpose.

In the past few years, there has been a lot of talk about sustainable development. We all want the effect of our development assistance to persist even after the project is complete, which is the only way that poor people will improve their lives. When we talk about sustainable development some organisations tend to be rigid. I was told that an NGO, whose name I will not mention, wanted to know how the material would be replaced in twenty years before approving a project to provide tables and chairs for a school! In my opinion, that is pushing the concept of sustainability a little too far.

The world of humanitarian aid is a changing world. We try to make rules to ensure that we get the maximum results with the money invested. However, with rules also comes heavy bureaucracy. Our governments and their team of officials have mastered the art of finding ways to complicate things. The forms needed to request a grant are so complicated now that some organisations have full time specialists dedicated to completing the grant request forms and to finding out how they can comply with the requirements of such and such a grant program. Some non-governmental organisations actually fall into the same trap. The administrative burden is such that more and more budgets are allocated to administration. We need to know how to read their financial statements to make sure the percentage of the money dedicated to the administration remains reasonable.

The major policies established by our industrialised countries are made in such a manner that when they announce financing to help a country, very often, after natural disasters such as in Haiti, they request that the biggest part of the money be spent here to keep our economy rolling and not the one of the devastated countries. Canada had such a policy until 2007. More recently the Canadian government has linked the Foreign Affairs Department to economic development. The Canadian International Development Agency (CIDA) has been included in the Department of Foreign Affairs and Development! Now our humanitarian help is linked to the economic development of Canada! Also worth mentioning is that countries that were promised large sums complained of having received only a small portion of the money promised.

As helping the needy is more popular than ever, large corporations have understood that they can benefit from this trend. Some travel wholesalers are now offering tourists going to Southern countries, tours with a "community" aspect. For example they will offer you to stop in a school to see the kids in their classroom singing their national anthem especially for you. Those who never had the opportunity to see what's going on outside their all-inclusive hotels like these stops because they find it touching. Personally I think that is absolutely indecent that each day some kids have to become part of the scenery to satisfy the tourists. It is not because these children are poor that we have to turn them into a tourist attraction. Such behaviour is no more acceptable abroad than it would be here.

A few years ago, during a familiarization trip for travel agents, a very well-known travel wholesaler brought two hundred fifty travel agents to an orphanage. As the vast majority of the group were women, they were touched by these young orphans. For an hour, they looked after the children; they held them in their arms, trying to communicate with them despite the language barrier, before putting them down on the floor when suddenly the signal to leave was given. These poor kids must surely have felt abandoned all over again. Fortunately, at least on that occasion, the gifts that the travellers brought were discreetly handed to the management of the orphanage and not directly in front of the children as was too often the case.

All is not rosy in the world of humanitarian aid. But there is some hope. Many people want to help and they will not let these administrative hurdles stop them. We have to find a way to help without being caught up in all this government red tape and that of the big NGOs.

In the Province of Quebec alone, over fifty international cooperation organisations offer internships abroad and look for volunteers. Most of them are members of the AQCOCI (Quebec Association of International Cooperation). It then becomes possible to work with local organisations that want to provide help abroad. On their website in Canada, each province has this type of organisation, which regroups those who work at the international level. I guess it is the same in the United States. On their websites you can see the list of members and you will be able to find the organisation that suits your needs. With a little work, you will find a way, your way, to change lives.

SPECIAL THANKS

I would like to thank all the men and women who devote their time to helping others. This book would not have been possible without the dedication of the members of the Rotary Clubs overseas who make sure that the projects are carried out as planned and that the money is spent for the purpose it was given. Thanks also to the clubs here in North America who devote themselves to fundraising. The money raised is always used to help those who need it the most.

The Rotary Foundation of Rotary International leverages these funds by multiplying up to 3.5 times the money donated by the members. Without all these people at the different levels of the organisation who give selflessly, none of this would have been possible.

P.B.

INDEX

You liked this book…

Invite the author to meet your group for a conference:

For information and conferences:
info@editionsmundo.com

Les Éditions
Mundo

Les Éditions Mundo
223 Versant Nord Boulevard, Quebec City, QC, G1X 3V5
418 626-1308

ALBUM

...worth thousand words
...endship credits.

...author, proudly posing in front of the Institute in Peru.

...g a convenio at La Curba, Peru.

The Agricultural Institute building in Peru.

Classroom in Peru: bamboo walls with tissue to cut out the dust.

The water tower built in the middle of the village of Cojimies.

A street in Cojimies which is flooded at every high tide.

Sister Diane Fortier, the author and Claude Martel inaugurating the water system in Aguacate, Ecuador.

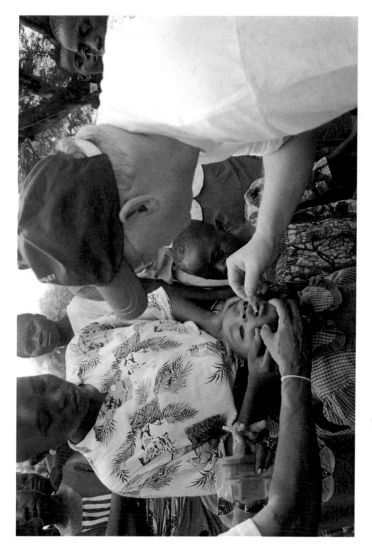

The author while vaccinating a child against Polio.

View of a village in the Douala islands, Cameroon.

A Warf on an island in the Ouri River, Douala, Cameroon.

Peter Smith vaccinating a fisherman's child.

Our taxi in the plantation in Cameroon.

TTree plantation in the Gobi desert.

A Tourist Camp in the Gobi Desert in Mongolia.

A traditional yurt.

With a nomad family in their yurt, Gobi Desert.

The Gobi Desert.

Sikh newly weds accompanied by the bride's mother.

Serge Poulin and the author giving blankets to a group of orphans in India.

Bamboo house building at Hogar de Cristo.

Our bus in Africa for Polio NID.

African women waiting for their child to be vaccinated.

Katrin Rhodes with a child and his Polio adapetd bycicle.

Serge Poulin and Paul Beaulieu in front of the Taj Mahal, India.

A sales person with her child on a sidewalk in Delhi.

Printed in Quebec
April 2015